CliffsN

T0090739

The House
of Mirth

By Bruce Walker

IN THIS BOOK

- ■ Probe the Life and Background of the Author
- ■ Preview the novel in the Introduction to the Novel
- ■ Examine in-depth Character Analyses
- ■ Explore the significance of the work with Critical Essays
- ■ Reinforce what you learn with CliffsNotes Review
- ■ Find additional information to further your study in CliffsNotes Resource Center and online at www.cliffsnotes.com

Ⓦ
WILEY
Wiley Publishing, Inc.

About the Author
Bruce Walker is adjunct professor of literature and technical writing at the University of Detroit Mercy in Detroit, MI. He earned a B.A. in English from Michigan State University in 1985. He has been a contributing editor to Gale Group's Literary Criticism Series, Contemporary Musicians, Newsmakers, and Encyclopedia of World Biography. He is also an author and editor of books for McGraw-Hill Children's Publishing.

Publisher's Acknowledgments
Editorial
Acquisitions Editor: Gregory W. Tubach
Copy Editor: Heather Wilcox
Glossary Editors: The editors and staff at Webster's New World Dictionaries
Composition
Indexer: TECHBOOKS Production Services
Proofreader: TECHBOOKS Production Services
Wiley Publishing, Inc. Composition Services

CliffsNotes™ The House of Mirth

Published by:
Wiley Publishing, Inc.
909 Third Avenue
New York, NY 10022
www.wiley.com

Copyright © 2003 Wiley Publishing, Inc. New York, New York

Library of Congress Control Number available from the Library of Congress.

ISBN: 978-0-7645-3716-5

10 9 8 7 6 5 4 3 2 1
1O/RR/QU/QT/IN
Published by Wiley Publishing, Inc., New York, NY
Published simultaneously in Canada

Table of Contents

How to Use This Book

CliffsNotes Wharton's *The House of Mirth* supplements the original work, giving you background information about the author, an introduction to the novel, a graphical character map, critical commentaries, expanded glossaries, and a comprehensive index. CliffsNotes Review tests your comprehension of the original text and reinforces learning with questions and answers, practice projects, and more. For further information on Edith Wharton and *The House of Mirth*, check out the CliffsNotes Resource Center.

CliffsNotes provides the following icons to highlight essential elements of particular interest:

Reveals the underlying themes in the work.

Helps you to more easily relate to or discover the depth of a character.

Uncovers elements such as setting, atmosphere, mystery, passion, violence, irony, symbolism, tragedy, foreshadowing, and satire.

Enables you to appreciate the nuances of words and phrases.

Don't Miss Our Web Site

Discover classic literature as well as modern-day treasures by visiting the CliffsNotes Web site at www.cliffsnotes.com. You can obtain a quick download of a CliffsNotes title, purchase a title in print form, browse our catalog, or view online samples.

You'll also find interactive tools that are fun and informative, links to interesting Web sites, tips, articles, and additional resources to help you. See you at www.cliffsnotes.com!

LIFE AND BACKGROUND OF THE AUTHOR

Personal Background

Edith Wharton, an American author and Pulitzer Prize winner, is known for her ironic and polished prose about the aristocratic New York society into which she was born. Her protagonists are most often tragic heroes or heroines portrayed as intelligent and emotional people who want more out of life. Wharton's protagonists challenge social taboos, but are unable to overcome the barriers of social convention.

Edith Wharton was born Edith Newbold Jones on January 24, 1862, in New York City to George Frederic Jones and Lucretia Stevens Rhinelander Jones. Her family on both sides was established, old-money New York business aristocracy. Her ancestry was of the best English and Dutch strains. Edith had two older brothers: Frederic Rhinelander Jones (Freddie), sixteen years older than her, and Henry Edward Jones (Harry), eleven years older. Edith was raised in a brownstone mansion on West Twenty-third Street in New York City. The Jones family frequently took trips to the country and to Europe. From the beginning of her life, Edith was immersed in a society noted for its manners, taste, snobbishness, and long list of do's and don'ts.

Education and Early Work

Edith did not attend school; according to the custom of the day for well-to-do young women, she was taught at home by her governess and tutors. She became proficient in French, German, and Italian. The books in her father's large library became her passion. Edith was fascinated with stories and began composing them herself when she was a child; she called the process "making-up." Her parents did not initially encourage her writing; after Henry Wadsworth Longfellow recommended that several of Edith's poems be published in the *Atlantic Monthly* magazine, however, her parents recognized her talent and had a volume of her poems (entitled *Verses*) privately published. A year later, when Edith was only sixteen years old, she completed a 30,000 word novella entitled *Fast and Loose*, a story about manners that mocks high society.

At the age of seventeen, Edith was immersed in her books. She spent her time studying, reading, and writing and was indifferent to people her own age. Worried about Edith, her parents decided that she should make her debut in society. Despite her natural shyness, she was a social success. In August 1882, at the age of nineteen, Edith became engaged to Harry Stevens, a prominent figure in New York society. By October of the same year, the engagement was broken as a result of meddling by the mothers of the engaged couple.

Married Life

On April 29, 1885, Edith married Edward R. "Teddy" Wharton, a friend of her brother. Teddy, who was thirteen years older than Edith, was from a socially acceptable Boston family. The Whartons settled in New York City and soon purchased a home in Newport, Rhode Island. Teddy's inherited income made it possible for the couple to live in New York and Newport, and to travel to Europe frequently. In 1902, they moved into their mansion, "The Mount," in Lenox, Massachusetts. Having collaborated with architect Ogden Codman on the book *The Decoration of Houses* (1897), Edith provided input regarding the design of the mansion as well as the interior decoration.

Though they were intellectually and sexually incompatible, the Whartons lived a companionable and expensive life, traveling back and forth between Europe and the United States. During the first years of Edith's marriage to Teddy, he was a companion to her and secured her position in the aristocratic society that she denounced, yet valued, throughout her life. Soon, however, events began to cloud their marriage. As Edith's writing abilities increased, so did her reputation. During the 1890's Edith wrote short stories for *Scribner's Magazine*, published *The Valley of Decision* (1902), a historical novel, and *The House of Mirth* (1905). She spent a considerable amount of time with would-be and genuine literary personalities and Teddy found himself in the background of Edith's life. His health and mental stability became progressively worse and required increasingly prolonged therapeutic trips to Europe. In 1907, the Whartons settled in France in the fashionable Rue de Varenne. While Edith's marital relationship began to fall apart, she continued to write. Her tragic love story, *Ethan Frome*, was published in 1911 to much success and acclaim. Eventually, Edith and Teddy began living apart, and in 1913, Edith divorced Teddy because of his unstable mental health and acts of adultery. Edith was also guilty of adultery. She had an affair with Morton Fullerton, a journalist for the *London Times* and friend of Henry James. (James, an American novelist, was a lifelong friend. His writing style, known as *American realism*, influenced Edith's writing.)

The French Years

After her divorce, Edith continued to visit the United States to retain her American citizenship, even though she chose to live in France. During World War I, Edith established two organizations for war refugees. She also made several visits to the French front where she distributed medical supplies and made observations from which she wrote war essays influencing Americans to support the Allied cause. Edith's war essays appeared in the book, *Fighting France, from Dunkerque to Belfort* (1915). As a fundraiser she organized *The Book of the Homeless* (1916), an illustrated anthology of war writings by well-known authors and artists of the time. Edith won the French Legion of Honor and was awarded many decorations by the French and Belgian governments for her contributions to charity. She continued her charitable efforts after the war.

In 1919, Edith purchased two homes in France: the chateau Ste. Claire in Hyeres, and the Pavillon Colombe, located north of Paris. Because she felt as though she had been cut off from the life she knew before the war, she was anxious to re-establish friendships and stability and began entertaining well-known literary personalities.

Edith continued to write until her death in Hyeres, France, on August 11, 1937. She was buried in Versailles in France. All of Edith's papers and unfinished work were given to Yale University with the stipulation that certain of them not be released until 1968.

Career Highlights

After publishing her first volume of short stories, *The Greater Inclination,* in 1899, Edith produced numerous novels, travel books, short stories (including many ghost stories), and poems.

Edith is perhaps best known for her novels depicting New York aristocratic life and the complicated struggle of the individual with the conventions of a powerful, and triumphant, moneyed class.

Edith received much acclaim for her lifelong devotion to writing. She is considered one of the leading American authors of the twentieth century. Because of her humanitarian endeavors and contributions to literature, Edith became the first woman to receive an honorary doctorate from Yale University in 1923, and in 1930 she was elected to the American Academy of Arts and Letters.

INTRODUCTION TO THE NOVEL

Introduction to the Novel

Wharton's novel is alternately described as a satire of New York City's wealthy and a tragedy about a physically attractive woman whose beauty causes men to desire to possess her and women to be jealous of her. *Tragedy,* in the classical sense, relates the downfall of a powerful individual that is brought on by his or her own arrogance or "hubris" (impetuous behavior brought on by excessive pride). The story of Lily Bart's descent from a former ingénue, still beautiful at the age of twenty-nine, to a destitute and haggard woman in her early thirties is certainly a tragedy of sorts, but Lily's tragedy is not so much borne out of her own hubris than it is caused by the unwavering attitudes of a society that is both desirous and envious of her beauty and spirit—facts that prevent the novel from being considered a tragedy in the classical sense of the genre. The tragic elements of *House of Mirth,* however, serve as convenient plot devices for Wharton in that they enable her to structure the novel's story much like a tragedy while never adhering entirely to the genre's structure.

The book's satirical elements are in many ways more pronounced than its resemblance to classical tragedy. The spoken observations of Lawrence Selden serve as one way by which Wharton is able to lampoon some of the seemingly absurd strictures of the wealthy class. Selden's character, however, is two-faced in the contempt he feels for the wealthy and his simultaneous desire to live among them. Lily is far more honest with herself—and Selden—when she defends the rites and conspicuous consumption of the wealthy as a way of life that she has been raised to accept and consider normal. Lily, however, also recognizes that the wealthy are able to follow their rules in an arbitrary fashion when she inadvertently crosses Bertha Dorset. Lily's ironic observation that it takes money to associate with the wealthy in order to play cards, tip, and dress appropriately is tragic in relation to her situation at the time, but also is consistent with Wharton's satirical tone. Perhaps the most significant aspects of Wharton's satire are the social-climbing Simon Rosedale and the Wellington Brys. Both parties are unpolished, nouveau riche newcomers to New York society. Their acceptance is contingent upon their learning the manners and customs of the wealthy. In Bry's case, however, he is much better accepted into society—particularly the European set—for simply being himself than is his pretentious and climbing wife.

The House of Mirth is often compared to the novels of Wharton's contemporary Henry James in their depiction of America's idle wealthy classes and the social codes to which they adhere. The novel is also compared favorably with the social novels of Upton Sinclair *(The Jungle)* and Theodore Dreiser *(McTeague* and *Sister Carrie)*. This writer also finds similarities between *The House of Mirth* and Stephen Crane's *Maggie: A Girl of the Streets*. Each of these novels indicts the hypocrisies of American value systems of different social classes. Such value systems, these writers hint, are antithetical to the promise of the American dream, which is a common theme of writers of the Gilded Age (a term used to describe the opulent America of the 1870s; the term is taken from the title of a novel written by Mark Twain and C.D. Warner that satirizes the era). Following such social codes without question, at best, leads to unrealized loving relationships; at worst, this adherence to convention can lead to the unnecessary concentration of wealth within a small-minded minority of a nation's population, as well as the pointless deaths of those needlessly trapped in impoverished circumstances.

Brief Synopsis

Lawrence Selden, a bachelor lawyer, views the exquisitely beautiful Lily Bart, a socialite who is expected to inherit vast sums of money from her wealthy aunt, and who is further anticipated to marry a man of vast wealth. Lily is twenty-nine years old and worries that her physical beauty is fading, which means that her chances for marrying an eligible wealthy man are also becoming slimmer. An orphan, Lily lives with her wealthy aunt, Mrs. Peniston, a miserly woman who refuses to give her niece an allowance.

Selden and Lily retire to Selden's apartment for tea and discuss the relative drawbacks to womanhood. Lily reveals to Selden that her manner has served to put off a potential mother-in-law, who has since sent Lily's prospective fiancé to India. Both Selden and Lily agree that the social functions they attend are boring affairs. Upon leaving Selden's apartment, Lily meets Simon Rosedale, a bachelor whose wealth continues to grow staggeringly, but whose presumptuous demeanor Lily finds repulsive.

Lily attends a weekend party at the country home of Judy and Gus Trenor, where she attempts to cement an engagement to the wealthy—and boring—young bachelor Percy Gryce. Lily turns her attentions to Selden, but finds that she has competition from Bertha Dorset, a married guest who has designs on Selden. Lily and Selden have a conversation in which it is decided that he is not wealthy enough to marry Lily. In the meantime, a bitter Bertha sabotages Lily's chances with

Gryce by shocking him with the knowledge that Lily plays cards for money. On a ride to town, Trenor tells Lily that he will invest money for her with no financial risk.

Lily is approached by a cleaning woman who has recently been fired from the building where Selden lives. Believing that Lily is the woman responsible for writing love letters to Selden, the woman wishes to sell the letters to her. Lily purchases the letters and discovers that they have been written by Bertha. In the meantime, Trenor's investments on Lily's behalf are paying off, and Rosedale continues trying to court Lily. Grace Stepney, Lily's cousin, is embittered by Lily's removal of Grace from a dinner party attendance list, and proceeds to tell Mrs. Peniston that Lily has been gambling and spending extravagantly. She also tells Mrs. Peniston that there are rumors that Lily is receiving money from Trenor, in effect making her a "kept woman."

Judy has also heard of the financial arrangement between her husband and Lily, and disassociates herself from Lily. Lily attends a social function at the home of Mr. and Mrs. Wellington Bry, two nouveau riche socialites. She poses in a *tableau vivant,* and her beauty is made apparent to all who attend. Selden professes his love for Lily, but she rebuffs him. The following evening, Lily meets with Trenor. Trenor feels that Lily owes him her physical affections for his financial assistance. Feeling violated, she leaves, and spends the night with Selden's cousin, the virtuous and physically undistinguished Gerty Farish, a kindly and charitable woman who has recently discovered that she is in love with Selden. The following morning, Lily determines that she will repay Trenor. She rebuffs another proposal from Rosedale and waits for the arrival of Selden. She discovers that Selden has gone to Europe and receives an invitation to join the Dorsets on a Mediterranean cruise.

During the cruise, Lily is a success with the European crowd, much to the dismay of Bertha. Bertha wishes to employ Lily as a means to distract her husband, George Dorset, while she engages in a flirtation with Ned Silverton. When Silverton and Bertha miss a train back to where the Dorsets' yacht is docked, Dorset and Lily return without them. Bertha returns to the yacht at seven o'clock the following morning. In order to excuse her absence, she insinuates that Lily and Dorset parted without her and Silverton in order to indulge in their own flirtation. Lily is told she must not return to the yacht.

The European stories regarding Lily's activities reach America and Mrs. Peniston, who dies leaving only $10,000 to Lily, a legacy that will take some time before being fulfilled. Rejected by her friends for the perceived indiscretion with Dorset, Lily finds work with the Gormers. Bertha, however, befriends Mattie Gormer, and Lily is soon out of work. She then finds work as a secretary to Mrs. Norma Hatch, a divorcée and recent addition to New York's wealthy elite. Norma has designs to marry Freddy Van Osburgh, a member of Lily's previous social group. Fearing charges of impropriety, Lily quits her job. She works, ineptly, at a millinery shop, and is laid off. Her mounting bills and increasing sleeplessness cause her to rely on chloral (chlorinated ethyl alcohol) in order to rest and forget her financial worries.

Lily resumes her contact with Rosedale, who offers to marry her if she uses Bertha's letters to Selden to even the score with Bertha. After some consideration, Lily begins to take the letters to Bertha, but she has an attack of conscience and visits Selden instead. She deposits the letters into the flames of a fire in his apartment. Neither Selden nor Lily can profess their love, and she leaves his apartment. The following morning, Selden realizes that he still loves Lily. He goes to her boardinghouse to tell her, but is greeted by Gerty, who tells her cousin that Lily has overdosed on chloral the night before and is now dead.

List of Characters

Lily Bart A physically beautiful woman of fading youth and frivolous nature. An orphan, she is taken in by the least wealthy of her relatives, Mrs. Peniston. Raised by her mother to believe that her beauty would restore wealth to her family, Lily has learned no practical skills nor developed any of her innate talents. Instead, she shows a knack for putting herself into morally and socially compromising situations, as well as being unlucky in cards and financial matters. Despite such personality drawbacks, however, Lily adheres to a strict code of behavior that prohibits her bettering her own situation at the expense of another.

Lawrence Selden A middle-class attorney who outwardly loathes the upper class but secretly aspires to belong to them. Selden realizes that his income is not sufficient to realize his dreams of marrying Lily, but he eventually proposes to her anyway. His fear of the judgment of the wealthy social class that has outcast Lily causes him to convince himself that he no longer loves her. When he realizes that he does indeed still love her, it is too late.

Gerty Farish   Selden's cousin, a pure-hearted young woman who labors for a living and does charity work in her spare time. Possessing neither physical beauty nor money, she secretly harbors a love for Selden while remaining loyal and steadfast in her assistance to Lily.

Carry Fisher   A twice-divorced woman with a young child who assists the newly rich to find their place in society by instructing them in manners and customs, as well as introducing them to a select group of the wealthy social class. She also assists Lily when the latter needs work and financial assistance.

Bertha Dorset   A cold-hearted, conniving woman who cuckolds her husband, George Dorset, and sabotages Lily's marital opportunities with Percy Gryce. She later uses Lily's unaccompanied late-night return to the Dorsets' yacht with Dorset as a device to cover her own indiscretion with Ned Silverton. Lily possesses letters written by Bertha to Selden, but refuses to use them against either of the pair.

George Dorset   Bertha's husband, a cuckold who is smitten with Lily. Lily, however, refuses to consider Dorset a potential candidate for marriage, as such an action would validate Bertha's lies about her.

Simon Rosedale   A Jewish businessman who is also in love with Lily. He is new to New York society and is decidedly rough around the edges, despite the administrations of Carry Fisher. Rosedale wishes to marry Lily until she is surrounded by scandal. He renews his proposal, provided Lily uses Bertha's letters to Selden to blackmail Bertha. Lily instead burns the letters.

Gus Trenor   Married to Judy Trenor, Trenor is an unattractive, insecure man who uses his ability to make money to seduce women outside his marriage. A heavy drinker, he is crass, rude, and sometimes boorish. He invests his own money on behalf of Carry and Lily, but expects a return of physical affection on his investment.

Judy Trenor   A superficial society wife who does not mind her husband's indiscretions but shuns any woman who accepts financial favors from him.

Mrs. Julia Peniston   Lily's aunt, a miserly woman who is easily shocked. When she hears that her niece is gambling, she cuts her inheritance to $10,000.

Grace Stepney   Lily's cousin who sabotages Lily's chance at receiving a significant inheritance from Mrs. Peniston.

Mr. and Mrs. Wellington Bry   New additions to New York society, Bry is accepted for his brash, uncouth demeanor, while Mrs. Bry is looked down upon because of her pretentious and obvious nature.

Mr. and Mrs. Van Osburgh   A wealthy couple with four unattractive daughters and a son, Freddy. Their daughter, Gwen, weds Lily's cousin, Jack Stepney.

Ned Silverton   A pathetic aesthete and chronic gambler, Silverton writes poetry that is presumably bad while relying on his sisters to support him financially. He clamors for a patroness, first with Bertha, and then with Mattie Gormer.

Freddy Van Osburgh   The heir to the Van Osburgh millions, he is targeted for marriage by divorcée Norma Hatch.

Mattie Gormer   An employer of Lily who is befriended by Bertha—a friendship resulting in Lily's dismissal.

Mrs. Norma Hatch   For a while, an employer of Lily. Hatch is a wealthy divorcée whose designs on Van Osburgh cause Lily to quit her job.

Nettie Struther   A young woman who was the beneficiary of Lily's one and only act of charity. Upon holding Nettie's baby, Lily realizes the lost hopes of her youth.

Mrs. Haffen   A cleaning lady who worked at the apartment building owned by Rosedale. She rescues the Bertha's letters to Selden, one of the building's tenants, and sells them to Lily—all with Rosedale's knowledge.

Character Map

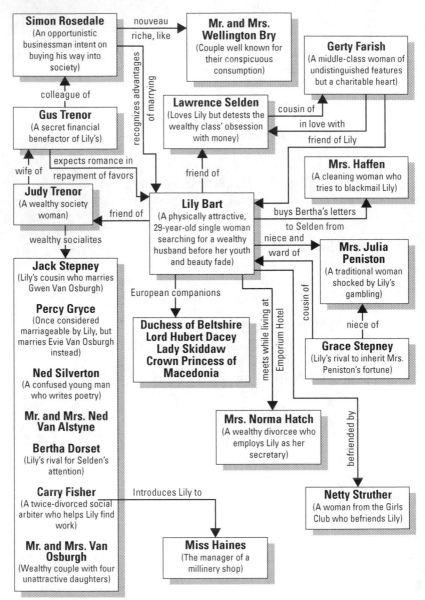

CRITICAL COMMENTARIES

Book 1
Chapter I

Summary

Set in New York City in the first decade of the twentieth century, the novel begins at Grand Central Station on a Monday afternoon in early September. At the train station, Lawrence Selden is approached by a casual acquaintance, Lily Bart. Lily has two hours to spend before her train arrives, and recruits Selden to entertain her. The pair leaves the station and travels to Selden's apartment building, *The Benedick.*

Over tea in Selden's apartment, Lily reveals her desire to have rooms of her own. She acknowledges that Selden's cousin, Gerty Farish, lives in an apartment, but shares the opinion of most society women—that only governesses, widows, or unmarriageable women live in apartments.

The pair's conversation turns to reasons why Selden seldom visits Lily at her residence in her aunt's—Mrs. Peniston's—house. Selden acknowledges that he is not a suitable suitor for Lily, or, at any rate, that he does not visit often because he is aware that Lily is not interested in him romantically. Lily rebukes Selden for presumptuously attempting to initiate a romantic engagement with her, and reveals that she has long considered Selden a confidante. She also reveals that she knows her female peers regard her as tiresome, and are beginning to become more obvious regarding their opinion that she should marry.

The two smoke cigarettes, which Lily lights from the end of Selden's, giving him cause to admire her beauty. They discuss the merits of collecting rare and first-edition books. Lily asks Selden if he minds not having enough money to purchase the books he wishes to own. He confesses that he is not a "saint on a pillar," indicating that he wishes to have more money than he earns. The conversation turns to what a man may choose to do in contrast to what a woman is forced to do regarding marriage as an economic arrangement.

Lily and Selden discuss the impending weekend party at the Trenor's country estate at Bellomont, and discuss the necessity of her attending society parties in order to meet eligible men, despite the fact that she and Selden agree that the functions are boring. She refuses Selden's offer to escort her back to the train station, and leaves his apartment alone. As she leaves, she sees a cleaning woman on the stairs. She perceives that the cleaning woman is staring at her, perhaps wondering what Lily's business was in Selden's apartment. She dismisses her thoughts concerning the cleaning woman's opinions.

Literary Device

As she leaves the apartment building, she is greeted by Simon Rosedale, whom Wharton describes as "a plump rosy man of the blond Jewish type." Rosedale questions Lily as to her business at the Benedick, and she lies that she is there to visit her dressmaker. Rosedale reveals that he owns the Benedick and knows of no tenants who make dresses. He offers her a ride to the train station, but she opts to take a passing hansom instead.

Commentary

Lily is twenty-nine years old, which is considered old for a single woman of the era. While admiring Lily's physical attractiveness, Selden wonders if she has colored her hair while he appreciates that "everything about her was at once vigorous and exquisite, at once strong and fine."

Wharton reveals that Selden is as interested in Lily's "discretions . . . almost as much as her imprudences." Lily's beauty is remarked upon from Selden's perspective. He compares her appearance to the comparative plainness of female passersby. Wharton goes on to describe the women as exemplars of the "dinginess, the crudity of this average section of womanhood" in order to differentiate Lily's beauty from the remainder of humanity. Wharton describes Selden's thoughts on Lily's attractiveness as an indicator that "a great many dull and ugly people must, in some mysterious way, have been sacrificed to produce her." Later, Selden admires the "streak of sylvan freedom in her nature that lent such savour to her artificiality."

Character Insight

Wharton indicates that Lily is still subject to the whims of her culture, however, when she has Selden notice Lily's blushing when he invites her to visit his rooms: "Her colour deepened—she still had the art of blushing at the right time." The remark reveals that Lily, while a maverick in some ways, will yield to the restrictions of her social class out of either habit or nature. Wharton furthers this perception by having Lily negatively remark on Gerty Farish as an unmarriageable woman who lives in "a horrid little place, and no maid, and such queer things to eat. Her cook does the washing and the food tastes of soap."

While Lily apologizes to Selden for the insult on his cousin, she confesses that Gerty "is free and I am not." Selden reinforces this perception when he envisions the links of Lily's sapphire bracelet as "manacles chaining her to her fate," which he believes makes her "the victim of the civilization which had produced her."

The different opportunities and lifestyle choices between men and women is furthered when Lily and Selden discuss marriage. Lily states that no one would mind if Selden attended a dinner in a worn coat, but that a woman is expected to be well-groomed and pretty, and that "if we can't keep it up alone, we have to go into partnership."

She visits the Benedick, the apartment building that is the dwelling place of Selden and that is owned by Rosedale. The name of the building, as Rosedale states, refers to bachelorhood. (Benedick is the bachelor in Shakespeare's *Much Ado About Nothing*.) Rosedale's acknowledgement that he knows the meaning of the building's name only because he owns it can be interpreted to mean that Rosedale can only know culture by buying it. This interpretation of the exchange between Rosedale and Lily underscores the previous conversation between Lily and Selden concerning the possession and collecting of rare and antique books. Likewise, a woman of culture such as Lily may also be possessed or owned by a person with the requisite income.

Literary Device

The refined appearance and carefree lifestyle of Lily is contrasted with the cleaning woman she sees on the stairs outside Selden's apartment. Their encounter also foreshadows Lily's eventual downfall.

Glossary

book-muslin with gigot sleeves   a light cotton fabric, once used to cover books, that was fashioned into sleeves that ballooned from below the shoulder to the forearm.

hansom   a two-wheeled covered carriage for two passengers.

La Bruyère   Jean de la Bruyère (1645–96), a French essayist and moralist.

bezique   a card game resembling pinochle, but using a double deck of sixty-four cards comprised of two of each card above the six.

Book 1
Chapter II

Summary

Riding in the hansom on the return trip to Grand Central Station, Lily considers the societal dictates that have forced her to lie to Rosedale. She believes that she has erred in three ways. The first was to impulsively visit Selden's apartment. The second was to lie to Rosedale; she considers lying better than telling the truth that she was alone with a bachelor inside his apartment. The third error was her refusal of Rosedale's offer to give her a ride back to the train station. Had she accepted the offer, she believes Rosedale would have been a willing conspirator in concealing her impropriety.

Wharton reveals that Rosedale had exhibited romantic designs on Lily in the past—designs that Lily thwarted due to his presumptuous entry into New York society. Rosedale had used a business associate's debt to him as a means to attain invitations to social events. Rosedale was shunned, as was the business associate, Jack Stepney, who wrangled the invitations for him. Judy Trenor, the wife of wealthy financier Gus Trenor and a leading member of society, recounted to Stepney (later revealed to be a cousin of Lily's) that Rosedale "was the same little Jew who had been served up and rejected at the social board a dozen times within her memory." Though rejected by Judy and her ilk, Stepney continued his attempts to integrate Rosedale into society, appearing with him and attractive females from society's fringes in fancy restaurants where Rosedale paid Stepney's tab.

On the train, Lily spots the wealthy bachelor Percy Gryce. She maneuvers to sit next to him after discovering that he is also bound for the house party at the Trenors. Gryce, however, is frightfully boring to Lily, forcing her to resort to engaging him in conversation about his collection of early American artifacts. This tactic proves fruitful, and Gryce regales her with stories of his latest acquisitions.

Gryce is a recent addition to New York society. He and his overbearing mother arrived from Albany after the death of Gryce's father. His wealth and availability for matrimony make him one of society's most eligible bachelors. Gryce's wealth derives from his father's patent on a device "for excluding fresh air from hotels."

Gryce and Lily are joined by Bertha Dorset, wife of George Dorset, an obnoxious, self-centered woman who is of slighter stature than Lily. Bertha asks Lily for a cigarette, and Lily disingenuously behaves as if she doesn't smoke in an effort to impress Gryce.

Commentary

Lily considers the social precepts she must follow burdensome. She wonders why a female can "never do a natural thing without having to screen it behind a structure of artifice." She acknowledges to herself that she has placed herself in Rosedale's power by lying about her visit to the Benedick, a power she feels he may use against her in the future.

Society's low regard for Jews displayed in the first chapter is elaborated upon in the second chapter. Wharton writes that Rosedale "had his race's accuracy in the appraisal of values" and continues that he believes being seen in public with Lily will enhance his social standing, as many might interpret her company as an indicator that he, too, is invited to the Trenors' house party. In addition, Wharton characterizes Rosedale as an opportunist who knows how to use his acquaintances to his financial advantage. Lily views the combined "artistic sensibility and business astuteness" traits of Rosedale as stereotypical traits of the Jewish race.

If Rosedale is an opportunist, Gryce is portrayed as a bore whose only defining characteristic—his book collection of Americana—is passed down to him from a wealthy uncle. This characteristic causes Lily to recognize Gryce as an individual lacking self-confidence.

Glossary

cutting a book   the necessary practice of slicing open the paper folios of books and magazines in order to read both printed sides.

oubliette   a concealed dungeon with a trap door in the ceiling as its only opening.

Sarum Rule   the pre-Reformation, Latin liturgy that is the source of the Anglican religion.

Book 1
Chapter III

Summary

After an evening of playing bridge at the Trenors', Lily retires to her room. She stops on the stairs to take in the opulent Trenor house, and notices Bertha engaging Gryce in conversation. She envies the married Bertha for her ability to talk to men and discard them with no regard. Because Lily and Gryce are both marriageable, Lily knows she cannot treat him in the same fashion.

When she enters her room, Lily compares her lot in life to that of Gerty Farish. She does not believe that she has been equipped to cope with the inconveniences of Gerty's life, which she believes includes garish wallpaper and the "squalid compromises of poverty." Lily feels that she requires a luxury that is her own, a recent change in attitude from the previous comfort she felt in relying on the hospitality of others. She has come to the realization that the hospitality of others has come at a personal cost, and that she has been required to "pay her way" by participating in card games that she cannot afford.

Wharton reveals that Lily has developed a weakness for bridge, a card game for which she has neither talent nor luck. Although she has won substantial amounts in the past, the monies she won were never banked against future losses, but spent imprudently on jewelry and fine clothing. On this particular evening, Lily has lost all but twenty dollars that she has brought with her, in contrast to Judy and Bertha, who both have won large amounts of money.

Lily dresses for bed without notifying her maid that she is doing so, a rudeness she rationalizes as fitting due to the fact that she has been "long enough in bondage to other people's pleasure to be considerate of those who depended on hers." Lily contemplates that she and her maid are in the same circumstances with the exception of one major difference: The maid is paid on a regular basis.

Lily observes lines developing on her face, which she first blames as an anomaly of the electric light in her bedroom; the lines, however, remain in candlelight. She then blames the lines on her monetary and marital worries. She wonders if her worries were caused by her own actions or if they were her destiny, and recalls the circumstances of her upbringing, which Wharton depicts as a consistent pattern of living beyond the family's limited means.

Character Insight

Lily recalls her social debut at the age of nineteen, which was an extravagant affair. The reader learns that the nineteen-year-old Lily knew nothing about the value of money when she berates her mother for not supplying fresh flowers for luncheon. She repeats her request to her father, who sarcastically laughs at her and tells her that she should order twelve hundred fresh flowers each day. During this exchange, Mr. Bart reveals that he is financially ruined.

Her father's bankruptcy and death prompts Lily and her mother to pay extended visits to wealthier relatives. It also gives Lily the resolve to marry into wealth by cultivating her beauty as well as the social tact necessary to attract wealthy and eligible men. Lily, however, is not as mercenary as her mother. Lily considers her physical attractiveness as "a power for good, as giving her the opportunity to attain a position where she should make her influence felt in the vague diffusion of refinement and good taste." She dreams of marrying into European nobility by wont of her beauty and her refined tastes.

After her mother's death, Lily is taken in by her father's wealthy and widowed sister, Mrs. Peniston. It is revealed that she is not the wealthiest of Mr. Bart's relatives, and that her motivations are not necessarily selfless. The narrator tells the reader that "It would have been impossible for Mrs. Peniston to be heroic on a desert island," which can be interpreted to mean that her motivation is simply to *appear* charitable to impress others. The companionship of the two women is a convenience for Lily until she finds a husband, but Lily considers her aunt to be financially well off but miserly when it comes to her niece. Mrs. Peniston refuses to give Lily a regular allowance, and instead chooses to grant her irregular monetary sums.

Lily's resolve to marry wealth is cemented by her realizing that she cannot live on the sporadic payments she receives from Mrs. Peniston. Such monies will not pay her dressmaker's bills and gambling debts.

Commentary

Wharton provides important details about Lily's past. Her family was once relatively well off, but a combination of economic downturns and financial mismanagement led to eventual bankruptcy. Lily, always beautiful, was told by her mother that the family's fortunes would be regained through her physical attractiveness.

The reader learns the details of Lily's youth, a life of money, European travel, and servants. Lily's mother is remembered as young and vivacious, while her father is seen as middle-aged, tired, and bald, even though he was only two years older than his wife. It is revealed that he struggled mightily to provide for his wife's extravagant lifestyle. The father is demonized by his wife and society at large for not consistently earning enough money to keep his family in the comforts to which it had been accustomed. His wife, however, is admired as a "wonderful manager" of money who always seemed to create the illusion that the Bart family possessed more wealth than it actually did. Any protest from Mr. Bart would result in a reproach from his wife that it would be considered "living like a pig" if her demands were not met.

Character Insight

Mrs. Bart's view of money overshadows any love she might have felt for Mr. Bart. This is revealed when Wharton relates that he "no longer counted" to his wife, and that "he had become extinct when he ceased to fulfill his purpose." Mrs. Bart's mercenary attitude toward her husband is summed up when she tells Lily, "You are sorry for him now—but you will feel differently when you see what he has done to us." Lily harbors hopes of marrying into wealth, yet considers herself better than her mother because she believes that her refined cultural tastes will serve as valued cultural enhancements—a belief Wharton belittles when she reveals that Lily's sense of culture is limited to pictures, flowers, and sentimental novels.

Glossary

Cole's Voyage of Life   a series of engravings by Thomas Cole (1801–48) depicting rural New York landscapes. Copies of the engravings were inexpensive, and ownership of the engravings was considered middle-class.

Quirinal   the Palazzo del Quirinal, built as the Roman summer home of the popes, eventually housed offices of the Italian government.

mauvaise honte   a disingenous display of shame used defensively to protect the actor from chastisement rather than out of an honest sense of remorse.

Book 1
Chapter IV

Summary

The following morning, Lily is summoned by Judy to assist her in some secretarial duties. Judy gossips with Lily about the twice-divorced Carry Fisher and Lady Cressida Raith. The latter woman is married to a London clergyman, and divides her time between gardening and charity work in the slums of London's East End. Judy had considered it a coup when she was able to introduce Lady Cressida to New York society, but was disappointed when Lady Cressida reveals herself to be the "moral one," which can be interpreted as "boring."

Judy also confides that Bertha is angry with the Trenors for failing to convince Selden to attend their house party. She has an idea that Gryce will be a suitable substitute for Bertha's attentions, an idea that Lily resists. Her resistance is answered with Judy's admission that Gryce was invited for Lily's benefit. The two women discuss the nature of the Dorsets' marriage. Their conversation turns to strategizing Lily's winning of Gryce's heart and money.

Lily observes the courtship of her cousin, Stepney, and Gwen Van Osburgh, a wealthy, heavy-set woman with a less-than-engaging personality whom Stepney considers "reliable as roast mutton." Lily recognizes that Gryce and Gwen are similar in that he has a nondescript personality and she has a nondescript appearance. As Lily has made up her mind that she will win over Gryce, she is approached by the newly arrived Selden. Their reunion, however, is abruptly interrupted by Bertha.

Commentary

The reader is told that Lily feels "an affinity to all the subtler manifestations of wealth" even as Wharton presents a foreshadowing of Lily's eventual banishment from society. Judy's request for Lily's secretarial assistance heightens Lily's feeling of dependence and servitude.

Changing perceptions in high society are made evident when the narrator recounts Judy's remark that there is "a divorce and a case of appendicitis in every family one knows." This comment is in reference to Carry, a twice-divorced woman who borrows money from Judy's husband, Gus Trenor. The arrangement between Carry and Trenor, while merely suspected by Judy, foreshadows a similar arrangement that will exist between Lily and Trenor.

Judy compares Lily to Bertha, and concludes that Bertha is the "nastier" of the two, which she imagines will result in Bertha's "always getting what she wants in the long run." Likewise, the narrator lampoons Carry's embracing of such causes and interests as municipal reform, socialism, and the Christian Scientist religion as indicators of the dilettantism of the upper classes.

The courtship of Stepney and Gwen parallels Lily's designs on Gryce. Lily believes that Stepney's lot is easier; all he has to do is remain quiet and he will be able to marry into the wealthy Van Osburgh family, whereas she must "calculate and contrive, and retreat and advance, as if I were going through an intricate dance, where one misstep would throw me hopelessly out of time."

Wharton reveals an underlying hypocrisy in Lily's character. As an outsider, she recognizes the shortcomings of the rituals of the wealthy. But as she resolves to marry Gryce, she becomes more accepting, "a stealing allegiance to their standards, an acceptance of their limitations, a disbelief in the things they did not believe in, a contemptuous pity for the people who were not able to live as they lived."

Glossary

parterres   ornamental garden areas in which the flower beds and paths form patterns.

Engadine   valley of the upper Inn River, East Switzerland, that was the site of many resorts.

crepe de Chine   a soft, rather thin crepe, usually made of silk, used for blouses, lingerie, and so on.

chary   not taking chances; careful; cautious.

Book 1
Chapter V

Summary

Lily attempts to further her designs on Gryce by accompanying the Trenors' daughters to church. She believes that Gryce will see how beautiful she looks while peering through long eyelashes over a hymnal and wearing a modest gray dress, and will fall hopelessly in love with her.

In an act of rebellion intended to increase Gryce's longing for her, however, Lily purposely misses the omnibus that takes the group of churchgoers to Sunday services. Instead, she interrupts a private conversation between Selden and Bertha, much to the delight of the former and the consternation of the latter.

Lily then sets out on foot for the church, hoping to catch Gryce returning from services. She is met by Selden, who surmises that Lily has designs on Gryce. Gryce does indeed return from church on foot, but as part of a group led by Lady Cressida that also includes the Trenors' daughters. Selden, recognizing that their earlier conversation about Americana was due to Lily's interest in snaring Gryce, offers to further his tutelage at length that afternoon.

Commentary

In this chapter, Wharton further satirizes the lives and attitudes of New York society. Lily misses the omnibus that takes the group to church services in order to increase Gryce's longing for her, but the action may also be interpreted as Wharton's attempt to point out the hypocrisy of a social group that attends church on a regular basis without practicing Christian teachings. Her narrator points out that society may be scandalized by the divorces of Carry, but that it will forgive such indiscretions if the remarriage is into greater wealth.

Book 1
Chapter VI

Summary

The chapter begins with Lily and Selden venturing out-of-doors for a prolonged conversation. The exhilaration she feels is compared to the only time Lily felt that she had been in love, with Herbert Melson. A man possessing good looks but little income, Melson eventually married an older sister of Gwen. Lily tempers her nostalgia by acknowledging that the handsome young man aged, put on weight, and became a man who incessantly related anecdotes about his children.

Wharton describes Selden as an intellectual of dark features and impressive height. Lily admires him because he possesses a sense of superiority over the mannerisms of the wealthy. He tells Lily that he has come to the Trenors' party specifically to see her.

Lily intends to use Selden's presence as a prop for her intentions for Gryce. She supposes that spending time with Selden will either relate to Gryce that she is not desperate for his proposal, or it will incite Gryce to jealousy. Earlier that day, Lily had feigned a debilitating headache as a reason to miss an afternoon automobile drive to the Van Osburghs' estate. The headache was intended to elicit Gryce's sympathy, a ploy that Selden observed with much amusement.

The conversation between Lily and Selden revolves around their respective definitions of success. For Lily, it is "to get as much as one can out of life." For Selden, it is personal freedom. The couple discusses money. Selden states that, for the rich, money is like air; removed from the comfort of their surroundings, the wealthy gasp like fish out of water. Lily responds that, as an individual adverse to the ways of the rich, he spends much time socializing with them.

Selden responds that he considers Lily too worthy for many men of the upper class. Lily answers that perhaps she might perform great acts with the wealth she could receive from a rich husband. Selden tells her that she is pursuing wealth that ultimately will not make her happy, and asks her if she has considered that result. She confesses that she has, but considers his assessment much darker than her own.

The conversation puts Lily in a darker mood, and she challenges Selden to explain why he should draw the limitations of her aspirations to her attention when he has nothing to offer her as an alternative. He confesses that if he possessed an alternative, he would give it readily. This admission causes Lily to weep, although Selden is unsure if she is putting on an act. He attempts to better the situation by stating that it is natural for him "to belittle all the things" he is unable to offer Lily.

Lily responds that, in belittling the things Lily desires, Selden is belittling her. Their conversation leads to Lily's asking Selden if he wishes to marry her. "I shall look hideous in dowdy clothes; but I can trim my own hats," she tells him. Before the conversation can conclude, the pair observes a passing automobile. When Selden notes that the car is traveling in the wrong direction and cannot be the Trenor party, as they initially assumed, they both seize the opportunity to end the seriousness of their conversation. In answer to Lily's question, "Are you serious?" Selden responds that he was under no risk by being serious, implying that Lily would never consider a proposal from him.

Commentary

The conversation between Lily and Selden takes place in a natural setting in contrast to the opulent interior settings of previous chapters. A possible interpretation is that the relationship between Lily and Selden is consistent with the natural course a loving relationship should take rather than the artificial restraints placed upon courtships by the upper class. In the outdoors, away from the constrictions of society, Lily could draw "deep breaths of freedom and exhilaration."

The conversation between Lily and Selden indicates that both individuals are cowards. Selden allows his lack of wealth and disdain for the customs of the wealthy—a form of vanity—to prevent him from actively pursuing his love for Lily. Lily's desire for the fineries of society causes her to give Selden the impression that she could never be happy married to him.

Glossary

Omar Khayyám   Persian poet and mathematician; author of the *The Rubáiyát*.

jeune fille à marier   a young woman ready for marriage.

Book 1
Chapter VII

Summary

Lily returns to the Trenor household to discover that Gryce has departed. Judy tells Lily that Bertha retaliated against Lily for stealing Selden's attention by telling ruinous stories about Lily to Gryce. These stories include Lily's borrowing money to repay a gambling debt, as well as stories about her previous suitors.

Judy asks Lily to travel to the train station to meet her husband. Lily goes to the station to greet Trenor, whom she finds repugnant. Trenor tells her that he has just completed a lucrative deal with Rosedale, whose fortune he predicts will soon eclipse his own wealth.

On their ride back to his estate, Lily appeals to Trenor to help her invest her money in order to provide a small income for herself. He promises that he can earn her with a small fortune with no risk.

Commentary

This chapter displays the viciousness of society women toward one another. Bertha is angered because Selden shows more interest in Lily than in her, so she gossips with Gryce about Lily. In addition, when Carry remarks that Gryce has no knowledge of the laws, Bertha reassures the twice-divorced woman that he is well informed on the laws of divorce and has signed a bishop's petition against divorce.

Lily's manipulation of Trenor results in his promising to invest money for her. His less-than-honorable intentions are hinted at, however, when he allows himself to rest his hand on hers.

Glossary

malum prohibitum   a violation of social custom.

Doucet dresses   fashionable dresses designed by French dressmaker Jacques Doucet.

Book 1
Chapters VIII–IX

Summary

Lily receives the first dividend—one thousand dollars—from the investment made on her behalf by Trenor. Trenor tells Lily that she has already earned five thousand dollars from a tip he received from Rosedale. Lily continues to humor Trenor, which she believes is enough to repay him for his efforts. Her new friendship of convenience with Trenor is encouraged by his wife, Judy, who believes Lily keeps Trenor in high spirits. Judy places Lily in a favorable light in comparison to Carry, whom she characterizes as a "vulture."

Lily is willfully ignorant of the risks of the stock market. She also is ignorant of the derivation of the initial investment that Trenor has made for her when she assumes he has borrowed from her securities. She considers the money she earns through Trenor to be hers alone.

Lily's cousin, Stepney, and Gwen marry in an elaborate ceremony. At the wedding, Lily sees both Gryce and Selden. She still perceives Gryce as a potential suitor. She also meets with Selden's cousin, Gerty, a young woman of simple means and undistinguished appearance. The two women admire the jewels that are gifts to the newlyweds, including a large diamond pendant, which is Rosedale's gift.

Gerty tells Lily that she has heard Gryce will soon announce his engagement to Evie Van Osburgh, whom Lily considers to be the least attractive and interesting of the four Van Osburgh sisters.

A mildly intoxicated Trenor approaches Lily with the news that he has sold her stock as it was rising, and has a check for four thousand dollars for her. Lily pays little attention to Trenor, and is scheming to steal Gryce away from Evie. Trenor complains that Lily has been avoiding his household since he has begun investing money for her. Lily regards spending time with Trenor a reckoning for his helping her, and agrees to attend to Rosedale as a partial return of Trenor's favor.

Lily leaves Trenor and is confronted by Selden. She remarks that she envies Gerty's ability to romanticize what Selden must perceive as the garish and ostentatious wedding gifts. She continues: "I have never recovered my self-respect since you showed me how poor and unimportant my ambitions were." He responds that his purpose was to prove that "they were more important to you than anything else."

The exchange is interrupted by Trenor and Rosedale. When she appears ready to snub him, Rosedale reminds her of the lie she told him in Chapter I by commenting on her dress and asking if she had it made at the fictional dressmaker shop in the Benedick. She allows Rosedale to accompany her for a lemonade, and the man struts like a peacock in the presence of the beautiful Lily. She employs Rosedale as an escort into the conservatory, where she intends to discover the truth about the engagement of Gryce and Evie. She encounters Evie's mother, Mrs. Van Osburgh, who confides that the couple is engaged.

At the beginning of Chapter IX, Lily's aunt, Mrs. Peniston, returns home, and Lily weighs the advantages of staying with either her or the Trenors for the fall. She opts to stay with Mrs. Peniston to avoid the indebtedness to Trenor.

**Literary
Device**

Upon the opening of Mrs. Peniston's house, Lily once again encounters the cleaning woman she saw at the Benedick. This time, Lily is rude to the woman. The cleaning woman, Mrs. Haffen, later tells Lily that she and her husband have been dismissed from the Benedick, and that she has letters addressed to Selden that she is willing to sell to Lily. Lily realizes that Mrs. Haffen believes that the letters were written by Lily when, in fact, they were written by Bertha. Lily purchases the letters, intending to destroy them.

Mrs. Peniston presses Lily for details of the Stepney–Van Osburgh wedding, telling Lily that she has heard that Bertha is taking credit for the match between Gryce and Evie. Lily retires to her room, where she places the letters from Bertha to Selden in a box for future use.

Commentary

Lily's shallowness and acceptance of upper class rules is given ample consideration in Chapter VIII. Lily despises Gerty's acceptance of her lack of wealth, and disparagingly notes to herself that Gerty's brightly colored dress is offensive because "it is almost as stupid to let your clothes betray that you know you are ugly as to have them proclaim that you think you are beautiful." Lily believes that Gerty makes up for her lot as a simple woman of simple means by engaging in symphony concerts and philanthropy. Of course, Gerty is presented as a foil for Lily, who cannot perceive the beauty of a human being who appreciates culture, helps others, and accepts her economic situation without complaint.

Wharton further portrays Lily as shallow when she resolves to break up the engagement of Gryce and Evie. Lily is more interested in marrying the boring Gryce in order to be wealthy than in allowing him to marry Evie, a marriage that would be a good match for the pair.

Lily's use of Trenor and Rosedale continues to display her mercenary attitude toward men. Trenor is a means by which she secretly acquires money, and she views Rosedale as a potential supplier of future stock tips. In the meantime, however, she employs Rosedale as an escort into the conservatory, where she discovers the truth about Gryce and Evie's engagement.

Lily's feud with Bertha has resulted in Bertha's taking credit for making the match between Gryce and Evie. Originally resolved to destroy Bertha's letters to Selden in order to avoid a scandal, Lily instead decides to preserve the letters and possibly blackmail Bertha.

Literary Device

The return of the cleaning woman is perhaps the novel's weakest reliance upon coincidence. Regardless, Lily recognizes Mrs. Haffen from the Benedick in a scene that parallels their initial meeting The fact that Mrs. Haffen has letters that might benefit Lily requires a stretch of the reader's imagination.

Glossary

Paquin   a turn-of-the-twentieth-century female French designer.

ormolu   an imitation gold made of an alloy of copper and tin.

point de Milan   fine Italian lace.

Book I
Chapter X

Summary

Lily spends the autumn with Mrs. Peniston, enjoying the money she has earned from Trenor's investments. She gives money to Gerty's favorite charity, although she exhibits pride in her action.

Upon returning from Thanksgiving vacation in the Adirondack Mountains, Lily is visited by Rosedale. He invites her to the opera, telling her that Trenor intends to attend as well. He implies that Trenor may have less-than-honorable intentions for Lily and that he may have committed earlier infidelities. Rosedale asks Lily how her investments are doing. She is shocked that Trenor has spoken about their arrangement, but also believes that Rosedale might be able to help her financially, as well. She accepts Rosedale's invitation to the opera.

At the opera, Lily appears beautiful in new clothes. Trenor, somewhat intoxicated, accuses Lily of no longer seeking his company because she no longer requires his financial help. He insists that he would like to see her alone, and Lily agrees to meet him in Central Park the following afternoon.

Dorset enters the opera box and passes on Bertha's invitation to Lily to visit their house the following Sunday. Lily believes Bertha's letters to Selden give Lily the upper hand over Bertha.

Commentary

Lily mistakes the feeling of self-importance she gets when she gives money to Gerty for altruism. This feeling is contrasted with the way she feels at the end of the chapter when she considers her possession of Bertha's letters to Selden a fitting revenge for Bertha's participation in the successful pairing of Gryce and Evie.

Lily's naiveté shows in her handling of Rosedale and Trenor. Rosedale implies that Trenor is a philanderer, an inference lost on Lily. Rather than risk a scene with the intoxicated Trenor, Lily agrees to meet him— although he's indicated he is not interested in "talking."

Book 1
Chapters XI–XII

Summary

Wall Street hits a slump during the holiday season, and all investors, excepting Rosedale and Wellington Bry, suffer financial losses. Rosedale is rumored to have doubled his fortune, thus smoothing his path to acceptance in New York society. He has been friendly with Carry Fisher, who has been beneficial in introducing him to influential persons and to social customs. He desires, however, a more individualized woman in his life and has set his cap in Lily Bart's direction.

The narrator recounts a holiday party thrown by Mrs. Peniston to welcome returning newlyweds Jack and Gwen Stepney. Mrs. Peniston's cousin, Grace Stepney, had thought herself invited to the dinner, but discovered she had been removed from the guest list. She suspects that Lily is responsible for the slight, and the relationship between the two women becomes strained.

Seizing an opportunity to revenge her slight, Grace tells Mrs. Peniston about the rumors that are circulating about Lily and Trenor. Grace tells Mrs. Peniston that people are talking about an estrangement between Lily and Judy, a result of a flirtation between the younger woman and Trenor. Grace continues that people have been saying that Trenor is paying Lily's bills, including her gambling debts. This statement reveals to Mrs. Peniston that Lily is playing cards for money, an activity unheard of in Mrs. Peniston's limited purview. To further her point, Grace tells Mrs. Peniston that it was Lily's gambling that frightened Gryce away.

Grace also informs Mrs. Peniston that it is rumored that Lily has been seen with Dorset, another married man. She recounts that Evie had seen several expensive items of apparel that were being sent to Lily, indicating that Lily is spending extravagantly and beyond her limited means.

As Chapter XII opens, Lily has ingratiated herself with the Dorsets in the belief that mending fences with Bertha allows her to find "a subtler pleasure in making use of [an] antagonist than in confounding him." Lily spends much of her time humoring Dorset, an activity far simpler than keeping the increasingly difficult Trenor at bay.

Trenor's fortunes were negatively impacted by the stock market crash. Lily suspects that the rumors about her flirtation with Trenor may have gotten back to Judy, which may explain the woman's suddenly cold behavior toward her.

The Brys' newly acquired wealth prompts them to throw a large party at their estate with the assistance of Lily and Carry Fisher. Attending the party are Selden and Gerty, both of whom were invited by Lily. Gerty confides to Selden that Lily has donated three hundred dollars to Gerty's philanthropy, her Girls Club, and has convinced the other society women to contribute large amounts as well.

The party features a *tableau vivant* in which volunteers re-create famous scenes of art or history. Lily is featured as the subject of Sir Joshua Reynolds' *Mrs. Lloyd,* a depiction of such beauty that it elicits gasps of appreciation from the audience. The painting is known for displaying the voluptuous form of its subject in a transparent gauze gown while she carves her lover's name into a tree. Selden's admiration for Lily's portrait prompts him to think "for the first time he seemed to see before him the real Lily Bart, divested of the trivialities of her little world, and catching for a moment a note of that eternal harmony of which her beauty was a part."

While some in the audience are scandalized by the exposure of Lily's form, Selden is mesmerized. He looks forward to speaking with her for the first time after intentionally avoiding her since the Stepneys' wedding. The two walk outside, and Selden professes his love to her. The couple kisses, and Lily tells Selden to love her "but don't tell me so." She leaves him alone. Selden leaves the party, but not until he hears Trenor and Ned Van Alstyne discussing Lily's attractiveness.

Commentary

Wharton makes light of the cyclical nature of the financial markets by comparing Wall Street to playing Cinderella. Rosedale's nouveau-riche status is emphasized by his purchasing the estate of a family ruined by the stock market crash. The narrator further uses Rosedale's Jewish heritage to disparage him: "The instincts of his race fitted him to suffer rebuffs and put up with delays."

Mrs. Peniston is parodied as a slave to social custom when the reader learns that the veracity of Grace's accusations are not as important as the fact that the accusations are being made in the first place: "It was horrible for a young girl to let herself be talked about; however unfounded the charges against her, she must be to blame for their having been made." In such a closed culture, all individuals are guilty until proven otherwise.

The *tableau vivant* presented by Lily reveals her as a truly beautiful woman, capable of enchanting most men. When Selden approaches Lily following the display, she feels "the quicker beat of life that his nearness always produced . . . [For] the moment it seemed to her that it was for him only she cared to be beautiful." Her love for Selden, however, does not fit her designs for herself, and she leaves him after their kiss.

Trenor delivers the last lines of Chapter XII. First, he complains that Lily's *tableau* was too revealing of her figure, and, second, he insults the nouveau riche hosts of the party: "My wife was dead right to stay away: she says life's too short to spend it in breaking in new people."

Glossary

Girls Club   a social and/or exercise club for young, single female laborers.

tableau vivant   a parlor game in which a participant attempts to replicate a well-known piece of art, history, or literary scene.

Veronese   Paolo Veronese (1528–88), an Italian decorative painter famous for his ceiling painting of such scenes as the Last Supper.

Book 1
Chapter XIII

Summary

Lily awakens to find two messages at her bedside. She assumes both are related to her success from the previous evening. The first letter is from Selden, requesting to see her. She fears that Selden will once again propose marriage to her, but sends a reply consenting to meet him the following day. The second letter is from Judy, who also requests to see her that evening. The latter correspondence cheers Lily, because she misses her old friend.

When she arrives at the Trenor house that evening, she is led to Judy's study where Trenor is waiting to speak with her. He confesses to employing duplicity in arranging the meeting—Judy is not home that evening—which angers Lily. He implores her to listen to him, and blocks the doorway with a chair so that she cannot leave. He accuses her of intentionally making him look foolish as well as taking advantage of his better nature.

Lily appeals to Trenor's understanding of societal rules regarding a single woman visiting a man without a chaperone, but Trenor responds that he knows that she had visited Selden alone in his apartment. He tells her that he expects some type of repayment for the financial success he has brought to Lily, and she offers to repay him in kind. She also states that Trenor has done only what any true friend would do for another. He responds that he believes she must have accepted similar kindnesses from many other men. Following the insult, he tells Lily that he is "mad" about her.

As suddenly as he had become enraged, Trenor becomes resigned to Lily's diffidence. The narrator explains his reasons for dismissing Lily: "Old habits, old restraints, the hand of inherited order, plucked back the bewildered mind which passion had jolted from its ruts." She leaves and takes a hansom back home. On the way, she recognizes Gerty's apartment, and decides to pay Selden's cousin a visit.

Commentary

The peaceful feeling Lily experiences upon awakening is quickly dispelled by the realities of her existence. The admiration and awe that she had inspired the previous evening is the fleeting appreciation accorded only to objects of art, and the following day's adventures bring Lily back to the mundane and sometimes painful reality of her life. She must once again contend with the romantic intentions of Selden, and worries that she may have to dispel the rumors of her relationship with Trenor to Judy.

Her mercenary treatment of Trenor prompts him to ambush her in his wife's study, where he alternately chastises and pleads with her for her attention. As a businessman, the only personal commodity he has to offer is of a monetary nature—he recognizes that he is neither physically attractive nor clever, and he has used his talent for earning money as a means by which to keep Lily in his orbit. His scheming to bring Lily into a private conference reveals him to be a totally pathetic individual, albeit one whom Lily used shamelessly to attain her own financial goals.

Literary Device

Lily's need to feel pure again leads her to stop at Gerty's apartment building. Lily desires to visit Gerty in order to receive her reassurances and compassion. The reader may also conclude that Wharton intends this scene to indicate that Lily may herself recognize that her social downfall is inevitable.

Book 1
Chapter XIV

Summary

The chapter begins in Gerty's apartment where Gerty has spent the night dreaming after realizing that she has fallen in love with Selden.

Character Insight

The narrator explains Selden's upbringing. His parents' lack of wealth was balanced by their happiness with each other. Consequently, Selden has learned to appreciate a simple lifestyle and to disdain the accumulation of material possessions as "aimless profusion."

After his encounter with Lily the previous evening, Selden is certain that he is in love with her and that she wishes him to propose. Selden returns from Albany to New York City, where he goes to his club. There, Trenor entreats Selden to eat supper with him, which. Selden refuses. He receives Lily's note regarding the following day's meeting and is invigorated, assuming that Lily will accept his proposal.

Selden visits Gerty for dinner. The two discuss Lily until Gerty surmises that Selden is in love with Lily. Although heartbroken, Gerty does not reveal her feelings. She tells Seldon that Lily was to dine at Carry's home, and Selden excuses himself to see Lily there.

When he arrives at Carry's house, Selden is told that Lily has already left. A guest says that he heard Lily tell the hansom driver to take her to the Trenor residence, even though it is well known that Judy is away and Trenor is alone at their town house.

Selden leaves Carry's party and is joined by Ned Van Alstyne in his walk down the street. As they near the Trenor residence, the pair observes Lily leaving the house and Trenor standing in the open doorway. Van Alstyne swears Selden to secrecy, explaining that "appearances are deceptive."

Gerty blames Lily for stealing Selden's affections from her, and for possibly the first time in her life, she allows herself to feel hate.

Following her confrontation with Trenor, Lily arrives unannounced at Gerty's apartment. Although Gerty's first inclination is revulsion toward Lily, she receives her tenderly when she realizes that Lily is terribly upset. Lily is hysterical, proclaiming herself to be bad. Gerty tries to reconstruct Lily's evening to discover what is troubling her. She recounts that she knows Lily had dinner at Carry's home and that Selden went there to find her. The mention of Selden's name prompts Lily to ask Gerty if she thinks her cousin can ever again think highly enough of Lily to help her. Gerty struggles with the question but responds that she is certain Selden will help Lily.

Commentary

More than any other chapter in *The House of Mirth,* Chapter XIV reveals that the novel was written in a serial format. This style is evidenced by the nonlinear presentation of the chapter, in which Wharton backs up time in order to fill the reader in on the thoughts and feelings of Gerty and Selden as they evolve after the Brys' dinner party. The reader can then understand what is happening to Selden and Gerty prior to and during Lily's fateful visit with Trenor.

Character Insight

Gerty previously had enjoyed life and romance only secondhand. Her newfound love for Selden and her charitable disposition prompt her to share her good fortune with others. Gerty believes that her love for Selden is reciprocal because of his frequent visits, and that the two have attained a higher degree of sympathy through their mutual affection for Lily.

Literary Device

Gerty's drawing Lily into her charitable work at the Girls Club, and Lily's participation, serves as a foreshadowing of Lily's future economic plight. The narrator regards Lily as learning to view the economically disadvantaged as individuals rather than en masse.

Theme

The narrator uses Van Alstyne to point out the values of old-money New York socialites in two passages. In the first, he sums up the social values of the day regarding unmarried attractive women: "When a girl's as good-looking as that [Lily] she'd better marry; then no questions are asked. In our imperfectly organized society there is no provision as yet for the young woman who claims privileges of marriage without assuming its obligations." The second instance occurs when Van Alstyne accompanies Selden after leaving Carry's house. He points out the differences of architecture between old money, like the Trenors' home, and new money, like the Brys' estate. He disparages the ostentatious nature of the Brys' home and compliments the Trenors' more austere Corinthian style.

Book 1
Chapter XV

Summary

Lily awakens in Gerty's bed the following morning. When Gerty enters the bedroom, the closeness the two women shared the evening before is dispelled. Gerty has phoned Mrs. Peniston to inform her as to Lily's whereabouts.

Lily returns home to Mrs. Peniston. She determines that she will repay Trenor an amount that she estimates is nine thousand dollars. She requests a private conference with her aunt prior to Lily's appointment with Selden. Lily confesses to her aunt that she has financial worries as a result of clothing extravagances and gambling losses—while withholding from Mrs. Peniston the true extent of her debt—in the hopes that Mrs. Peniston will give her enough money to repay Trenor.

Mrs. Peniston expresses her intense displeasure at Lily's admission that she has been gambling—and that she has played cards on Sunday. On these grounds, she offers to give Lily only $1,000 to pay a dressmaker's bill.

Upset, Lily waits for Selden's arrival. She had initially hoped to find refuge in his company in the event Mrs. Peniston gave her the money to repay Trenor. Now, possessed with the knowledge that her aunt will not help her, she harbors hopes that Selden will marry her and enable her to put her troubles behind her.

Selden never arrives, however; instead, Rosedale pays Lily a visit. He boasts that he is now among the wealthiest men in New York, and that he intends to take a wife to help him share in his fortune. He assures Lily that his wife shall have more than she ever desired, and certainly enough to make every other society woman jealous.

Recognizing that he is declaring his marital intentions, Lily protests that she has never meant to give him the impression that she was interested in him romantically. Rosedale responds that he is aware that she does not love him, but that in time her love of luxury, style, and amusement will force her to recognize that they will make a good business and social match. He also reminds her that she is not going to be young and beautiful forever. In addition, he makes an allusion to the confrontation she has had with Trenor the previous evening.

Lily responds that she would be "selfish and ungrateful" to accept Rosedale's proposal only to fulfill her financial obligations. She uses this as a ploy to ask for time to consider his offer, and Rosedale leaves. Despondent that Selden has not kept his appointment, Lily writes him a letter but, before she can send it to him, she reads in the evening paper that he has left New York on an extended cruise to Cuba and the West Indies.

She begins to write a letter to Rosedale, presumably to accept his proposal, but cannot bring herself to complete it. She receives a message from Bertha. The letter is an invitation to join the Dorsets on a Mediterranean cruise that is leaving the following day.

Commentary

Although the events of the previous evening have upset Lily, her first thoughts upon awakening are those of the old Lily, annoyed at the discomfort she has suffered by sleeping in Gerty's austere surroundings. This irritation indicates that she will never be comfortable without the luxuries to which she has become accustomed. It is certainly implied that she would not choose to turn her back on an affluent lifestyle.

**Literary
Device**

As Lily contemplates accepting Rosedale's proposal, she observes herself in the mirror. She recognizes that she is beginning to show signs of physical aging, and wonders, "when a girl looks old to herself, how does she look to other people?" She reconsiders Rosedale's offer, and the combination of her debts and her fears of looking older nearly induce her to write Rosedale to tell him that she has made up her mind to marry him. She cannot complete the letter, however, and is interrupted by the delivery of the invitation to join the Dorsets on their cruise.

Book 2
Chapter I

Summary

The chapter opens with Selden in Monte Carlo. He is accompanying the Stepneys, the Brys, Lord Hubert Dacey, and Carry. Selden is informed that Lily is also in Europe, where she is vacationing with the Dorsets, and that she has been causing a mild sensation. Carry tells Selden that Lily appears ten years younger, and that she has become a favorite companion of the Crown Princess of Macedonia. These revelations awaken Selden's hurt feelings over Lily, which surprises him as he believed he had recovered from his feelings of unrequited affection.

Carry and Selden go for a walk together, and she tells Selden that Lily once had prospects to marry a rich Italian prince during a visit to Europe five years earlier. She reveals that marriage documents were being prepared between the prince and Mrs. Peniston when Lily began flirting with the prince's stepson. Carry further gossips that Lily's current visit to Europe was prompted by Bertha's desire to have Lily distract Dorset while Bertha carried on a flirtation with Ned Silverton. Shocked and dismayed by the candid nature of the conversation, Selden excuses himself.

Upon catching the train back to Nice, Selden reemphasizes his resolve to avoid contact with Lily. As he boards the train, however, he is confronted by Lily, who is accompanying the Dorsets, Silverton, and Dacey to Nice in order to dine with the Duchess of Beltshire. He notices that Carry's assessment that Lily's beauty had blossomed while in Europe is correct.

In Nice, Silverton tells Selden that the trip to Nice was prompted by Lily's manipulation of Dorset. This manipulation, he tells Selden, was performed in open view of Bertha, who refused to hear any ill words against Lily. Silverton confides to Selden, however, that such actions could not help but injure Bertha's pride. In the meantime, Bertha's flirtation with Silverton reaches its apex when Selden observes the pair hailing a carriage for what the reader can assume will be a romantic tryst.

Commentary

Theme

Wharton uses Selden's observations to satirize the idleness of the wealthy Americans in Europe. They are depicted as spending the majority of their time in indecision over where to eat. Furthermore, the wealthy are shown to be more interested in where they might be observed eating and with whom as opposed to what they will actually eat.

Carry divulges the pretentiousness of the upper class when she relates her observations of the Brys to Selden. She tells him that Bry would fare better in his attempts to enter society if Louisa would let him indulge his personal style rather than putting on airs and constantly correcting her husband.

Character Insight

Carry tells Selden about Lily's courtship with the Italian prince and subsequent flirtation with his stepson to illustrate her belief that Lily "works like a slave preparing the ground and sowing her seed; but the day she ought to be reaping the harvest she oversleeps herself or goes off on a picnic." This statement not only reveals Carry's belief that Lily is her own worst enemy, but it also indicates to the reader that Lily really does not wish to marry for money rather than love.

Literary Device

Selden's chance meeting with Lily on the train to Nice gives Wharton the opportunity to foreshadow Lily's fate. Selden observes that Lily is "on the edge of something—that was the impression left with him. He seemed to see her poised on the brink of a chasm, with one graceful foot advanced to assert her unconsciousness that the ground was failing her."

Literary Device

Silverton's discussion with Selden concerning Lily's behavior in Sicily also serves as an opportunity for Wharton to foreshadow Lily's destiny. According to Silverton, Lily's open manipulation of Dorset has served to injure Bertha's pride, an injury that will eventually cost Lily a valuable friendship and lead to her downfall.

Glossary

gargote   a diner that is considered too downscale by the American travelers in Europe.

Book 2
Chapter II

Summary

The following morning, Lily awakens aboard the Dorsets' yacht, the *Sabrina*. She requests a meeting with Bertha but is rebuffed. Instead, Lily leaves the yacht to attend a breakfast with the Duchess of Beltshire.

On her way to breakfast, Lily encounters Carry, who offers Lily the chance to replace her as the Brys' social consort. She advises Lily to accept the position because she believes Lily is on the verge of social scandal. Carry reveals that the society writer Dabham has told everyone that he witnessed Lily returning alone with Dorset the previous evening after midnight. Lily protests that she and Dorset had waited for Bertha and Silverton at the train station, but the second couple never arrived.

Lily then encounters Dorset, who tells Lily that Silverton and Bertha did not return to the *Sabrina* until after seven in the morning. He relates Bertha's excuse, which includes a preposterous scenario of a carriage drawn by one lame horse. Suspecting his wife has been unfaithful, Dorset takes Lily's advice to seek Selden's legal counsel.

Lily speaks with Bertha, who tells a slightly different version of the story she had previously related to Dorset. When Lily notes the discrepancy, Bertha blames the inconsistency on her husband's "attack" of nerves. The two women engage in an argument during which it becomes apparent that Bertha is accusing Lily of seducing Dorset in order to mask her own infidelity.

Commentary

This chapter serves as a transitional section of the novel by showing the pettiness of society people in dealing with individuals of whom they are jealous. Bertha is prepared to destroy Lily's reputation because of perceived slights from Lily; in addition, Bertha attempts to cast aspersions on Lily in order to cover up her own infidelity.

Book 2
Chapter III

Summary

Selden receives Lily's telegram requesting his intercession on behalf of the Dorsets. Selden meets with Dorset and fears the worst for Lily's reputation. Lily remains aboard the *Sabrina* despite the tension between the Dorsets and Bertha's harsh treatment of Lily.

Lily goes to town and encounters Selden, who relates his concern for Lily's reputation. He worries that Lily is unable to defend herself socially from Bertha's wrath, and advises Lily to leave the Dorsets' yacht during a dinner hosted by the Brys. Lily asserts that she is in no danger, but Selden's fears are later realized when Bertha announces to the group that Lily will not return with them to the *Sabrina*.

Selden accompanies Lily from the dinner party, vowing to help her find a place to stay. He receives Stepney's permission to let Lily spend the night at their hotel provided that she not disturb Stepney's sleeping wife, Gwen, and that she leave by train the following morning.

Commentary

Character Insight

Selden's attitude toward Lily has transformed from smitten suitor to protector. He realizes that Lily's behavior has been reckless, but he also acknowledges that she is incapable of defending herself from the implications of being exiled by Bertha. Selden's later behavior is hinted at when Wharton reveals that he has developed a "sense of privilege" through his association with the Brys and Stepneys.

Literary Device

Perhaps nowhere else in the novel is Wharton as disparaging toward the wealthy social class as when she presents Selden's observations of the contrasts between Lily and the other dinner guests. She depicts the gossip columnist Dabham as a social parasite. She has Selden observe the "ideals of a world where conspicuousness passed for distinction, and the society column had become the roll of fame." Such is the society that will cast off one of its own regardless of the merits of the charges against her.

Book 2
Chapter IV

Summary

Lily leaves France and, under the auspices of the Duchess, goes to London. While she is in London, the Dorsets, Brys, and Stepneys return to New York with their own versions of Lily's exploits in Europe. Upon her return from London, Lily is told that her aunt and benefactor, Mrs. Peniston, has died. At the reading of the will, she is surprised to learn that Grace has been the left the majority of Mrs. Peniston's estate, and that Lily will receive only $10,000.

Lily is determined to use her inheritance to settle her debt with Trenor. She discusses the Dorsets' shunning her and her meek inheritance with Gerty. Rather than relate the actual details of the incident to Gerty, Lily tells her that an accusation is as good as the truth in society. The two go to lunch and are joined by Carry, who is glad to see Lily.

While dining with Gerty, Lily encounters Judy. She notices that Judy is cordial, but she also conspicuously refrains from asking Lily about her future and further neglects to express a desire to see her again.

Desperate for money, Lily goes to Grace to borrow money against her inheritance. Grace tells Lily that the estate will not be settled for some time. She refuses the request to borrow money against the inheritance on the grounds that Mrs. Peniston did not condone borrowing. Grace also tells Lily that Mrs. Peniston's meager allotment to Lily was intended as an admonishment for Lily's behavior.

Commentary

Literary Device

Wharton displays the shallowness of New York society by depicting the reading of the will as an episode of respect shown toward Lily—for as long as the attendees at the reading believe that Lily will be the sole benefactor. When she receives only $10,000, Lily notices an immediate change in their behavior toward her.

Book 2
Chapter V

Summary

Lily leaves Mrs. Peniston's house and once again meets Carry. She tells Lily that she has resolved her differences with the Brys, and is once again employed by them as their social advisor. She suggests that Lily perform similar duties for Sam and Mattie Gormer, another nouveau riche couple who know nothing of Lily's past and are eager to climb the social ladder. She tells Lily that the Gormers enjoy the company of actors and artists. The Gormers are also planning a trip to Alaska, and Lily agrees to accompany them as Mattie's social advisor.

Upon Lily's return from Alaska, Carry suggests to her that her troubles would be alleviated if she married. Carry says that Lily has two potential suitors, Dorset and Rosedale. She tells Lily that Dorset has confided to her that he is ready to divorce Bertha. Lily refuses to discuss any relationship with Dorset, and admits to herself that she despises Rosedale less than she had previously, but worries about entering a marriage not based on love.

Commentary

Character Insight

Lily reveals her own shallowness in her views of Rosedale. She considers him less repulsive for having attained the wealth he desired. This wealth also resulted in his being named to municipal committees and charitable boards, as well as being accepted to several exclusive clubs. The fleeting nature of society's favor, however, has shifted. While Rosedale has gained in favor, Lily's reputation had suffered since Rosedale's initial proposal. She begins to doubt whether Rosedale still needs her to fulfill his social aspirations, and if he still might love her enough for marriage.

Book 2
Chapter VI

Summary

Lily continues to work for Mattie and assist in the Gormers' social ascendancy. The couple begins to build an estate near the Dorsets', prompting Mattie and Lily to visit the building site often. During one of their visits, Lily is approached by Dorset, who apologizes for the events in Europe. She treats him with disdain, but feels some pity for him. Dorset is desperate for her friendship, but she dismisses him.

Literary Device

When Lily arrives at the Gormer estate, Mattie tells her that she has just met Bertha. Lily is struck by a sense of foreboding. This foreboding is realized as Lily recognizes an eventual increase in Bertha's influence over Mattie's tastes and behavior.

Lily struggles with increasing debt and resolves to marry Rosedale. Dorset makes a surprise visit to Lily. Lily realizes Dorset only wants to relate to her his own misery and is barely cognizant of her dire financial straits.

Lily encounters Rosedale at Carry's home. Carry tells Lily that Mattie has visited her in the company of Bertha, revealing to Lily that her tenure with the Gormers will soon come to an end. Once again, Carry emphasizes that the only way Lily can even the score with Bertha is to consent to marry either Rosedale or Dorset.

Commentary

Literary Device

In this chapter, we are introduced to the nameless child of Carry, who is contrasted with the presence of Rosedale. This scene will be echoed later with the baby in the arms of Nettie Crane Struther.

Carry very rightly warns Lily that Bertha continues to torment her because she fears that Lily might expose her affairs with Selden and Silverton. If Lily possesses wealth through marriage, Carry reasons, the power that comes with such money will render Bertha powerless.

Book 2
Chapters VII–VIII

Summary

While still visiting with Carry, Lily goes for a walk with Rosedale. Lily considers her past experiences of setting up courtships that never reach their fulfillment in engagement. She steels herself to not ruin her current opportunity with Rosedale.

She tells Rosedale that she will marry him, despite the fact that he has not repeated his proposal. He reveals that he had no intention of repeating the proposal, and she responds that she never meant her initial refusal to seem as if it were a final decision.

Rosedale admits his love for Lily, but also confesses that he does not wish to be associated with the scandal surrounding Lily and Dorset. He tells her that he does not believe the stories that he has heard about the affair, but that if he marries her while she is still surrounded with scandal, he will dash all hopes of societal acceptance.

Rosedale asks Lily why she hasn't attempted to get even with Bertha, and reveals that he knows she possesses the love letters that Bertha had written to Selden. He suggests that she use the letters to blackmail Bertha into backing Lily's aspirations. Such an action would put Bertha and Lily back on equal footing, and would enable Rosedale to marry Lily. Once they are married, Rosedale reasons, his wealth will protect her further from Bertha's scheming. Lily rejects Rosedale's plan, and he guesses that Lily is attempting to protect Selden, the recipient of the letters. Rosedale reminds Lily that Selden hasn't been much of a friend to her since the incident in France.

As Chapter VIII opens, Lily's fears that Bertha is undermining Lily's position with the Gormers are realized. Lily makes an infrequent visit to Gerty, who tells Lily that Silverton has once again taken up gambling and living far beyond his means. He also has been cast away from the Dorsets. Lily confides to Gerty that she hasn't been sleeping well, a condition she attributes to an impoverishment brought on by living with the wealthy. Later, it is revealed that Carry has lined up another position for Lily.

Gerty visits Selden and tells him about Lily's predicament. She asks Selden to assist Lily and he consents. He pays a visit to Lily's hotel only to find that she has moved to the posh Emporium Hotel, where she is now working as a secretary for Mrs. Norma Hatch.

Commentary

Wharton points out that the walk taken by Lily and Rosedale is ironically the same route taken earlier in the novel by Lily and Selden. At the onset of their walk, Lily arrogantly tells herself that she can transform Rosedale into a man deserving of her companionship.

Rosedale is a pragmatic individual. He tells Lily that he does not believe the stories he has heard concerning Lily and Dorset, but also confesses that "my not believing them ain't going to alter the situation." Later, he tells Lily that he desires social position, defending his admission by labeling his aspirations as a hobby, much as another man desires a stable of racing horses or a picture gallery. He further sums up the attitudes of New York society by telling Lily that, even if she is innocent of the accusations brought against her by Bertha, "Everybody knows what Mrs. Dorset is, and her best friends wouldn't believe her on oath where their own interests are concerned; but as long as they're out of the row it's much easier to follow her lead than to set themselves against it, and you've simply been sacrificed to their laziness and selfishness."

Character Insight

Rosedale's deduction that Lily is protecting Selden when she refuses to use the letters to blackmail Bertha may or may not be true. While Lily harbors a love for Selden, she also appears to reject the plan because of the sinister nature of such an act. While Lily may be vain and shallow, she seems here to be more interested in conducting herself in a proper manner. Another interpretation is that Lily rejects Rosedale's plan simply because it is Rosedale who proposes it. After all, Rosedale is not born to the customs of the wealthy class, and Lily naturally would be indignant toward and suspicious of any plan that he might concoct.

Despite the increasing hardships Lily confronts, Wharton continues to lampoon the wealthy social classes. Upon her realization that her tenure with the Gormers is ending, Lily contemplates the daily chores of the socialite, "drudgeries" that include "card-leaving, note-writing, enforced civilities to the dull and elderly, and the smiling endurance of tedious dinners." While Wharton is making a satirical point, Lily remembers those drudgeries with a degree of nostalgia.

Wharton explains Lily's rejection of Rosedale's blackmail suggestion. Her rejection is depicted as a noble action, albeit one that Wharton describes as the easiest action to take. However, Wharton tells the reader that Lily "had learned to live with ideas which would once have been intolerable to her" simply by listening to Rosedale's offer.

Gerty observes Lily's character, and finds her cousin is still trying to keep up appearances of wealth despite her dwindling financial resources. Gerty recognizes that, "Lily was not of those to whom privation teaches the unimportance of what they have lost." This observation is emphasized when Lily tells Gerty, "I always understand how people can spend much more money—never how they can spend any less!" during their conversation about Silverton's extravagance. She tells Gerty that living with the rich is an expensive proposition, requiring large tips, expensive clothing, and involvement in cards.

Character Insight

The conversation between Selden and Gerty reveals the selfless nature of the latter and the character flaws of the former. Selden has been avoiding contact with Lily due to the scandal with the Dorsets. He also negatively judges Lily for her quick intimacy with the Gormers. He finds it easier to negatively judge her for her patterns of behavior rather than to succumb to his previous feelings of love for her.

Book 2
Chapters IX–X

Summary

Lily is now working as secretary to the multiply divorced and wealthy socialite Mrs. Hatch at the Emporium Hotel. Hatch is the head of her social group, which includes Mr. Melville Stancy, Silverton, and Freddy Van Osburgh.

Selden visits Lily at the Emporium; he is uneasy and makes inappropriately defensive comments. He stridently offers to take Lily away from Mrs. Hatch and the Emporium. He tells her to room with Gerty until Lily's inheritance is paid. Lily tells Selden that she owes every penny of her inheritance. Selden is firm in recommending that Lily depart Mrs. Hatch's employ, but this firmness stiffens Lily's determination to stay.

In Chapter X, Gerty recommends millinery work to Lily—a position for which she seems suited as she has remarked that she can trim hats. Also, wanting to help Lily, Carry approaches Judy. Judy reacts violently, which baffles Carry. Carry gets Lily work at Mme. Regina's millinery shop, but Lily refuses to work on the sale floor modeling hats for fear of being seen by her former social circle; she instead goes to work constructing the hats. She is chastised by the forewoman, Miss Haines, for crookedly sewing spangles on a hat, but is comforted by the kindliness of Miss Kilroy, a co-worker.

Lily has begun to use Mrs. Hatch's prescription for chloral (chlorinated ethyl alcohol) in order to sleep. The pharmacist warns her not to increase the dosage. While filling the prescription, she encounters Rosedale. Rosedale and Lily go for tea, and Lily tells Rosedale her reasons for leaving the employ of Mrs. Hatch: She did not want to be perceived as assisting Mrs. Hatch's romantic designs on the wealthy Van Osburgh. Because Rosedale admits he has heard rumors of Lily's involvement, Lily expresses that she might as well have stayed employed with Mrs. Hatch.

Lily tells Rosedale that she is working for Mme. Regina, a revelation that shocks the wealthy financier. She also tells him that she owes her entire legacy to Trenor and others. Before he can offer to help her, Lily excuses herself from the table. Rosedale walks her back to her boarding room and asks to see her again. Lily graciously agrees.

Alone in her room, Lily contemplates using her inheritance from Mrs. Peniston to set up her own millinery establishment. From the proceeds, she reasons, she can pay back Trenor. Such a plan, however, she knows will take years. She blames Bertha for her misfortune, and wonders how long she can continue to resist the temptation to use the letters against her. She drugs herself and falls into a deep sleep.

Commentary

Style & Language

Wharton casts her satire toward the newly rich denizens of the Emporium Hotel. Wharton writes that Mrs. Hatch's daily life was a "jumble of futile activities" that, to Lily, has no rhyme or reason.

Because of Mrs. Hatch's unfamiliarity with the manners and customs of the New York social elite, Lily underestimates her as ignorant of social convention. In fact, Mrs. Hatch will eventually turn on Lily in much the same fashion as Bertha.

The narrator views the meeting between Selden and Lily as a lost opportunity for both characters. Had either of them risen above their social training to express their feelings, the narrator believes their differences could be put aside. Selden also displays his blinkered and superficial view of the world when he castigates Lily for working for Mrs. Hatch, which he calls "unconsciously placed in a false position." Wharton uses Lily's resolve to stay with Mrs. Hatch to display Lily's recognition of the hypocrisy of a social class that exiles its own but presumes to tell the exiled what they must do afterward.

Selden's conversation with Lily has served to do more harm than good in that his approach caused Lily to stiffen her resolve rather than see the wisdom of his message. The narrator states that Lily stayed in the employ of Mrs. Hatch several weeks beyond the time she should have left simply as a resistance to Selden's advice. However, Lily's attitudes toward the wealthy social class are becoming drastically altered, which she reveals when she tells Rosedale that she feels Van Osburgh "is not in the least too good for" Mrs. Hatch. Recognizing that her decision to quit the job was based more on her fear of societal opinion than on more practical financial concerns, Lily realizes that there was no real need to leave Mrs. Hatch.

Book 2
Chapter XI

Summary

Lily observes the traffic on Fifth Avenue, and sees Mrs. Van Osburgh, Evie, and the latter's new infant. She also sees Mrs. Hatch and Judy. Lily has been laid off from Mme. Regina's shop, a fate that she had anticipated.

Rosedale visits Lily. He offers to loan her the money to repay Trenor, but she refuses, telling Rosedale that she has nothing to secure the loan. He tells her that he is leaving for Europe for a period of several months, and would like to help her. He renews his offer to marry her with the implied provision that she set aside her differences with Bertha. Lily is touched by his declaration that he could position her where she "could wipe [her] feet on 'em!"

Lily considers using the letters to convince Bertha to allow Lily's return to society. The following morning, she devises her plan at a restaurant on Fifty-ninth Street. She goes home to retrieve the letters, and then heads to Bertha's home. On her way, however, she passes the street where she had strolled with Selden two years prior. She considers how Selden would judge her intended action to blackmail Bertha. She sees a light in Selden's apartment and enters his building.

Commentary

Lily contemplates the differences between beauty in nature and beauty in society. Social beauty, she believes, is hampered by material desire and moral scruples. She chafes at what Wharton describes as the "selfish despotism of society." Lily realizes that she lacks the moral constancy to succeed as a working-class woman, and admits that she is nostalgic for the life of the idle rich.

Lily considers her relationship with Selden, and realizes that she has squandered the love he once harbored for her. She also realizes that she has employed Selden as a moral compass in the past and once again gauges her actions according to his opinion of her.

Book 2
Chapter XII

Summary

Lily arrives in Selden's apartment and apologizes for the circumstances of their last meeting. Regardless, there is a distance between the two of them, a distance that Lily realizes is permanent. She admits her cowardice in turning down his offers of marriage, a cowardice borne out of her fear of living a less affluent life. She confesses to having made a mistake, a mistake she feels has caused Selden to judge her negatively ever since.

Literary Device

Lily asks Selden to remember her, and he responds by offering to help her. She asks Selden to remain her friend, and secretly deposits Bertha's letters into the open flames of Selden's fireplace. She says goodbye to Selden with an air of finality.

Commentary

Character Insight

Once again, Wharton points out that the differences between Lily and Selden could be laid to rest by an "immediate outrush of feeling." In this instance, however, Selden maintains his reserve and the moment passes despite Lily's admissions that she has taken great comfort in Selden's previous admissions of love for her. Rather than looking at her lovingly, however, Selden observes her with a look of "gentle understanding." While he no longer loves Lily, he still cares deeply for her welfare and well being. Lily, on the other hand, realizes that she once loved Selden but forfeited his love for superficial, monetary reasons.

Book 2
Chapter XIII

Summary

On her way home, Lily takes a seat in Bryant Park. She encounters Nettie Crane Struther, the young woman from the Girls' Club who had been the beneficiary of Lily's charity. Nettie is married to a motor-man, and is the mother of an infant daughter whom she has named in honor of Lily.

Lily retires to her boardinghouse, and goes through the remainder of her possessions. A maid brings her a letter, which contains the $10,000 legacy check. She considers how to spend the money to pay her bills, and realizes the loneliness of her solitude. She writes a check for repayment in full to Trenor as well as a bank deposit slip for the check.

She remembers the chemist's advice about using too much of the chloral prescription but does not heed it. She carelessly overdoses and drifts off into her final sleep.

Commentary

Wharton again has Lily realize the ironies pervading her life when Lily meets Nettie, a young woman whom Lily rescued from consumption with the money she had received from Trenor. Nettie represents the good that can come from helping the poor, and also represents the happiness that can exist in a life devoid of wealth. Nettie's naming of her baby after a character portrayed by an actress resembling Lily is both touching and representative of an individual's ability for rebirth—an ability that Lily is unable to recognize. Nettie tells Lily that she has missed Lily's name in the newspaper society pages, and declares that she hopes her daughter grows up to be like Lily, a comment from which Lily demurs: "Oh, she must not do that—I should be afraid to come and see her too often!"

Lily considers Nettie's story about marrying her husband, George Struther. She remembers Nettie telling her that "I knew he knew about me," referring to her presumed status as a "fallen woman." Lily realizes that Struther's faith in Nettie enabled him to love her enough to marry her, and that such faith was necessary for love and enduring happiness to exist. It was such faith that Lily exploited when turning down Selden's proclamations of love.

Character Insight

Whether Lily's chloral overdose is intentional or not is subject to debate. While she has seemingly exhausted all her opportunities, she has also received her legacy check early, enabling her to settle her debt with Trenor. Wharton writes that Lily is only interested in a deep sleep, and her tolerance of the drug must have certainly increased, requiring an extra dosage for the desired effect. The depiction of Lily's character throughout the novel, however, has been one of abject carelessness. It is most likely this character defect that ultimately results in her death—not suicide.

Book 2
Chapter XIV

Summary

The following morning, Selden decides to visit Lily. He has found the one word that he wishes to say to her. He arrives at her boarding-house to find Gerty, who tells him that Lily is dead. Cognizant of Selden's true feelings for Lily, Gerty leaves him alone with Lily's body. He finds the check written to Trenor, which confuses him. Selden also finds the letter he had written her expressing his desire to see her two years earlier. He recognizes his subsequent inability to maintain his love for Lily as an act of cowardice. He knows that he once loved Lily and that she once loved him, but that her background and his negative judgments of her lifestyle had conspired to keep them apart. He kneels by her bed in penance and to feel one last loving moment between them.

Commentary

The one word that Selden wants to tell Lily is, presumably, the word "love." It is the one word that is conspicuous by its absence throughout the novel—and remains unspoken until the book's final paragraphs. Selden realizes that he still loves Lily, and that their respective differences "had never been more than a little impalpable barrier between them."

Whereas Selden previously would have judged Lily negatively for having a financial transaction with Trenor, Wharton writes that, upon her death, "he felt only a taint of such a transaction." Wharton holds up Selden's cowardice as equally responsible for Lily's downfall and demise as her own actions. Because he feared social reprisal and personal rejection, he abandoned his love for Lily.

CHARACTER ANALYSES

Lily Bart

Lily Bart is a red-haired young woman of great physical beauty. Men are as drawn to her beauty as women are threatened by it. Raised by a mother who taught her the price of everything and the value of nothing and a father who lost and unsuccessfully endeavored to rebuild a family fortune, Lily is told by her mother that it is incumbent upon her to use her beauty in order to marry into wealth.

Lily Bart, for all her faults is a fully realized character. Her inability to manage money is attributed to attitudes she learned from her mother. Her inability to understand men is attributable to the fact that her father was consistently away at work in order to pay for his wife and daughter's extravagances.

When the novel begins, Lily is twenty-nine and still single. She has squandered several promising marriage opportunities, but feels she still can marry a wealthy man. However, she fears that her beauty may be fading along with the bloom of her youth.

At the beginning of *The House of Mirth,* Wharton depicts Lily as a shallow young woman. Despite Lily's frivolous and shallow nature at the novel's beginning, throughout the novel she displays the desire to act in an ethical fashion. While at first participating in charitable acts in order to feel good about herself (much like Mrs. Peniston—see below), she is eventually confronted with the positive results of her charity. She refuses the sexual advances of Gus Trenor, even though such an acceptance would render her bill paid in full. She declines to verbally defend herself against Bertha Dorset's accusations, believing that such a defense would only dignify Bertha's charges. Finally, she refuses to blackmail Bertha, an act that easily could have resolved all her financial problems.

Mr. and Mrs. Bart

Although the novel begins with Lily already orphaned, her parents are critical characters in her development. Her mother raises Lily with a sense of entitlement to wealth. Her father, portrayed as a tired shadow of a man who works ceaselessly to provide his wife and daughter with money, is never home long enough to give Lily an adequate male reference point from whom she can gauge other men. Instead, she is taught to gauge a man's worth by his wealth.

Chapter III presents a clear portrait of the family dynamic in which Lily was raised. Described by the narrator as "turbulent," the Bart household is a flurry of French and English maids, trips to Europe, extravagant spending sprees for clothing and material possessions, and discussions about money. Lily's mother is the dominant parent, youthful in appearance and able to "dance her ball-dresses to rags." She tells Lily that she had been "talked into" marrying Mr. Bart, a match she obviously regrets. She henpecks her husband into further extravagances by asking him repeatedly "if he expected her to 'live like a pig'" when he challenges her spending. When the family loses its wealth, she tells her daughter, "But you'll get it back—you'll get it all back, with your face."

Lily's father is described as a "hazy outline of a neutral-tinted" man whose presence in the household is relegated slightly above the positions occupied by "the butler and the man who came to wind the clocks." As an adult, Lily can recall no time when her father was not bald and beset with worry, even though he was only two years older than Mrs. Bart. In his efforts to return the family to prosperity, he works ceaselessly. Because of this, Lily's recollections of him consist mainly of hearing his voice asking the house servants about Lily's well-being after she has gone to bed. He works through the summer, and spends his weekends visiting with his wife and daughter on their holidays in Southampton. He also works while Mrs. Bart and Lily vacation in Europe. He eventually experiences complete financial ruin.

Despite the family's financial circumstances, Mrs. Bart insists on keeping up appearances. Her hiding of the family's misfortune results in her daughter's lack of knowledge concerning monetary matters. Following her husband's death, Mrs. Bart continues to live beyond her means. Two years younger than Mr. Bart, Mrs. Bart dies two years after his demise of "a deep disgust."

Lawrence Selden

Lily regards Lawrence Selden as her moral compass, a regard that is ill-advised. While he makes critical observations of the wealthy, he also rigidly and hypocritically adheres to their code of behavior—a code that he subsequently applies to Lily after Bertha falsely accuses her of seducing her husband.

Selden is revealed to be a collector of first-edition books, and the reader should draw the conclusion that Selden intends to collect Lily as another rare and beautiful object. While it is not doubted that he eventually comes to actually love Lily, he engages in such an infuriatingly indecisive and indirect approach while trying to court her that Lily is alternately flattered and insulted.

Selden can be dim in matters of love. He is unaware that his cousin, Gerty, has fallen in love with him, although such a fact should not escape him. When he finally makes up his mind to once again pledge his love for Lily, he is one day late.

Gerty Farish

Gerty Farish is an idealized depiction of American womanhood unspoiled by wealth and entitlement. A physically plain woman, she remains a steadfast supporter of Lily, despite the fact that she knows that her secret love, Lawrence, is instead in love with Lily.

Gerty's simple life would be considered "dingy" by Mrs. Bart's standards, and Lily herself disparages Gerty's lifestyle to Selden in Chapter I. Lily scoffs that Gerty is not "marriageable—and besides, she has a horrid little place, and no maid, and such queer things to eat. Her cook does the washing and the food tastes of soap."

Carry Fisher

Carry Fisher is a good character foil for Lily. She is an attractive, twice-divorced mother who can still travel in wealthy social circles as a woman who helps the newly rich understand the intricacies of society. She has also weathered the scandal of accepting financial advice from Gus Trenor, and Judy Trenor's subsequent wrath. When Lily faces scandal at Bertha's hands, it is Carry who provides her with employment opportunities with the Gormers, Mrs. Norma Hatch, and the milliner's shop. She also regularly supports Lily by inviting her to her house, where Lily will chance upon such marriageable prospects as Simon Rosedale.

Simon Rosedale

Perhaps the novel's most controversial depiction because of the blatantly anti-Semitic descriptions employed by Wharton to describe him, Simon Rosedale is nevertheless a fully realized character with both admirable and despicable qualities. Possessing enormous wealth and the potential to possess far more, he desires to marry Lily in order to expedite his entry into New York society. He continuously pledges his love for Lily, but also realizes that Lily has become a social liability. He offers her a solution—publicizing love letters from Bertha to Selden—albeit one that Lily cannot bring herself to enact: first, out of fear of exposing Selden's dalliance and, second, out of her revulsion to blackmail. The transaction by which Lily acquires the letters in the first place is most likely arranged by Rosedale, as he later indicates to Lily that he knows she possesses the letters. Rosedale subsequently offers to repay the money Lily owes Trenor, but Lily refuses on the grounds that a similar offer from Trenor got her into trouble in the first place.

Gus Trenor

A petty, vindictive man, Trenor also personifies the vanity and corruption of the wealthy. A physically unattractive man, he attempts to assist attractive young women in their financial affairs in order to compromise and exploit them. When he makes his initial offer to help Lily, it is clear to the reader (if not to her) that he will expect repayment in romantic favors.

Trenor is rude, often drunk, and boorish. He is allowed to behave this way simply because he is wealthy. His inability to manipulate Lily frustrates him because he is used to possessing whatever he desires.

Bertha Dorset, Grace Stepney, Judy Trenor

Bertha Dorset, Grace Stepney, and Judy Trenor are three women who are equally despicable in their treatment of Lily. The women are treated as co-conspirators within a grand cultural and social scheme to worship conspicuous consumption and moral hypocrisy.

Bertha is a major contributor to Lily's downfall by her eagerness to exact revenge on Lily—a revenge borne out of her jealousy of Lily's physical beauty and pleasant demeanor. Angry that Lily has bettered her in European society and eager to hide her infidelity with Ned Silverton, Bertha kills two birds with one stone by fabricating a story that Lily has seduced her husband, George Dorset. Thus ensuring Lily's scandalous society downfall, Bertha compounds her revenge by poisoning Mattie Gormer against Lily.

Despite Bertha's deceitful efforts to outcast Lily, Lily still could survive in society under the right financial circumstances. Grace Stepney, however, sabotages Lily's expected legacy from Mrs. Peniston. Because she rightly believes that her cousin has slighted her by removing her name from the guest list of an important social function, Grace reveals the rumors circulating about Lily to Mrs. Peniston. Mrs. Peniston reacts by pledging the majority of her fortune to Grace instead of Lily. This further complicates Lily's precarious financial situation by forcing her to ask her cousin for an advance on her inheritance—an advance that Grace refuses Lily.

Judy's rebuff of Lily cements the latter's intent to repay Trenor. Thus, Lily not only is broke because of the paltry legacy she receives from Mrs. Peniston, she also is deeply in debt. In addition, it is stated in the novel that Judy does not mind her husband's extramarital flirtations, but becomes incensed when other women—such as Lily and Carry—benefit from his financial skills.

Mrs. Peniston

After her mother's death, Lily is taken in by her aunt, Mrs. Peniston, a widowed sister of Mr. Bart whose wealth is overshadowed by other members of Lily's extended family. Mrs. Peniston takes in Lily because other family members shame her into it—she lives alone and cannot devise a legitimate excuse not to take charge of Lily.

Mrs. Peniston measures all time in terms of occurring prior or subsequent to her husband's death. According to the narrator, "She belonged to the class of old New Yorkers who have always lived well, dressed expensively, and done little else; and to these inherited obligations Mrs. Peniston faithfully conformed."

Mrs. Peniston's shortsightedness also allows her to be easily manipulated to reduce Lily's legacy. Knowing that Mrs. Peniston will disapprove of Lily's gambling, Grace reveals the truth about Lily's debts, thereby assuring that Grace will replace Lily in Mrs. Peniston's financial favor.

CRITICAL ESSAY

The Critics: *The House of Mirth* as Gilded

For three more critical essays, visit www.cliffsnotes.com/extras.

The Critics: *The House of Mirth* as Gilded Age House of Cards

Edith Wharton's *The House of Mirth* documents the moral bankruptcy of wealthy New York denizens during the waning years of the Gilded Age. This indictment of the culture that metaphorically eats its own reveals Wharton's opinions of such a society, as well as her views on the economic disparities in New York. Her handling of such subject matter prompted critic Alfred Kazin to note in 1941: "It is easy to say now that Edith Wharton's great subject should have been the biography of her own class, for her education and training had given her alone in her literary generation the best access to it." In fact, the passage from Ecclesiastes from which the book takes its title—"The heart of the wise is in the house of mourning, but the heart of fools is in the house of mirth"—indicates that Wharton considered New York society to be vain, petty, and foolish. Wharton's personal familiarity with her subject matter added the weight of tragedy to her often hilariously biting satire of the ways of the wealthy.

The Gilded Age, a term taken from the title of an 1873 novel by Mark Twain and Charles Dudley Warner, denotes a period "noted for political corruption, financial speculation, and the opulent lives of wealthy industrialists and financiers" (*Webster's New World College Dictionary,* 4th Edition). Wharton wrote *The House of Mirth* and, later, *The Age of Innocence* to expose what she knew about the social customs of the wealthy. In a letter to Dr. Morgan Dix, rector of New York City's Trinity Church, Wharton wrote: "Social conditions as they are just now in our new world, where the sudden possession of money has come without inherited obligations, or any traditional sense of solidarity between the classes, is a vast and absorbing field for the novelist."

The attitudes of the Gilded Age were still evident in New York society when Wharton serialized *The House of Mirth* in *Scribner's Magazine* from January 1905 to November 1905. Mary Moss, writing in 1906 in *The Atlantic Monthly,* described *The House of Mirth*'s depiction of New York society: "Mrs. Wharton has no colors too black, no acid too biting, for its unredeemed odiousness and vulgarity. She shows its sensuality to be mere passionless curiosity; she displays its cautious balancing of affairs so that reputations are preserved, not lost, in the divorce courts; her people, with regard to the quality commonly known as virtue, resembling rich defaulters who are lucky enough through a technicality to miss a term in jail."

In what is considered Wharton's first major literary effort, she is credited for presenting a successful blending of social satire and criticism. Critic Louis Auchincloss wrote in 1961, the novel "marks her coming of age as a novelist. At last, and simultaneously, she had discovered both her medium and her subject matter. The first was the novel of manners and the latter the assault upon the old Knickerbocker society in which she had grown up of the new millionaires, the 'invaders' as she called them, who had been so fabulously enriched by the business growth following the Civil War. . . . Mrs. Wharton saw clearly enough that the invaders and defenders were bound ultimately to bury their hatchet in a noisy, stamping dance, but she saw also the rich possibilities for satire in the contrasts afforded by the battle line in its last stages and the pathos of the individuals who were fated to be trampled under the feet of those boisterous truce makers."

According to Auchincloss, Wharton "had a firm grasp of what 'society,' in the smaller sense of the word, was actually made up of. She understood that it was arbitrary, capricious, and inconsistent; she was aware that it did not hesitate to abolish its standards while most loudly proclaiming them. She knew money could open doors and when it couldn't, when lineage would serve and when it could be merely sneered at." Auchincloss continued: "She realized that the social game was without rules, and this realization made her one of the few novelists before Proust who could describe it with any profundity."

CliffsNotes Review

Use this CliffsNotes Review to test your understanding of the original text and reinforce what you've learned in Wharton's *The House of Mirth*.

Q&A

1. Lily does not marry Dillworth because

   a. She discovered his family was bankrupt.

   b. He became jealous of Lily's flirting.

   c. His mother feared she would reset the family jewelry.

2. Lily stops working for the Gormers after

   a. They discover she is romantically linked with Simon Rosedale.

   b. Bertha Dorset poisons Mattie Gormer against Lily.

   c. Lily is compromised by Gormer.

3. Bertha Dorset maligns Lily's character in order to

   a. Mask Bertha's affair with Lawrence Selden.

   b. Get revenge on behalf of Judy Trenor.

   c. Mask Bertha's affair with Ned Silverton.

4. Gerty Farish is cousin to

   a. Lawrence Selden.

   b. Carry Fisher.

   c. Lily Bart.

5. Lily accepts the Dorsets' invitation to travel to Europe

   a. In order to court Ned Silverton.

   b. In order to find Lawrence Selden to accept his proposal.

   c. To help her forget her debt to Gus Trenor.

6. Gerty wishes to keep Lily's chloral overdose a secret because

   a. She suspects Lily was killed.

   b. Suicide was socially unacceptable.

   c. She is using Lily's death to further her romance with Selden.

7. Lily refuses to use Bertha's letters to Selden to help her cause

a. Because she believes blackmail is wrong.

b. She would then have no choice but to marry Simon Rosedale.

c. She secretly loves George Dorset.

8. Lily stops working for Mrs. Norma Hatch because

a. She doesn't want to encourage the impression that she is assisting Mrs. Hatch's romantic designs on Freddy Van Osburgh.

b. Mrs. Hatch has discovered that Lily has Bertha's letters to Selden.

c. Bertha Dorset, Gwen Stepney, and Judy Trenor have befriended Mrs. Hatch.

Answers: (1) c. (2) b. (3) c. (4) a. (5) c. (6) b. (7) a. (8) a.

Identify the Quote

1. "Gad, you go to men's houses fast enough in broad daylight—strikes me you're not always so deuced careful of appearances."

2. "There are bad girls in your slums. Tell me—do they ever pick themselves up? Ever forget, and feel as they did before?"

3. "Oh negative ones merely—what not to be and to do and to see. And I think I've taken them to admiration. Only, my dear, if you'll let me say so, I didn't understand that one of my negative duties was *not* to warn you when you carried your imprudence too far."

4. "I think it's just flightiness—and sometimes I think it's because, at heart, she despises the things she's trying for. And it's the difficulty of deciding that makes her such an interesting study."

5. "Isn't marriage your vocation? Isn't it what you're all brought up for?"

Answers: (1) Gus Trenor admonishing Lily in Book 1, Chapter XIII. (2) Lily addressing Gerty after the former was accosted by Trenor. (3) Bertha Dorset to Lily as they argue on the *Sabrina*. (4) Carry Fisher to Selden, concerning her fear that Lily is due to a downfall at the hands of Bertha. (5) Selden to Lily during their first conversation in the novel's opening chapter.

Essay Questions

1. Does the original epigraph for *The House of Mirth*—from the Old Testament Ecclesiastes 7:4: "The heart of the wise is in the house of mourning, but the heart of fools is in the house of mirth"—help to explain the novel's intentions? Why or why not?

2. Do Wharton's themes of blindly adhering to social conventions during the Gilded Age in *The House of Mirth* share similiarites with contemporary society? Be specific, and try not to limit your discussion to the differences between the upper, middle, and economically disadvantaged classes.

3. Many critics view *The House of Mirth* as an indictment of the Gilded Age's objectification and social entrapment of the female of the species. Do you agree or disagree with this assessment? Be sure to use specific examples from the book to support your response.

4. If Lily had survived the chloral overdose and married Lawrence Selden, would the pair have enjoyed a successful marriage? Why or why not?

5. Wharton's depiction of Simon Rosedale has caused her to be labeled an anti-Semite. Is her portrayal of Rosedale meant to incriminate and disparage American Jews or is it merely an attempt to satirize the nouveau riche?

6. Much feminist criticism has been written about Wharton's novel. Does *The House of Mirth* deal exclusively with feminist issues? Support your arguments by discussing Lily's use of tobacco, and her statement in the first chapter: "What a miserable thing it is to be a woman!"

Practice Projects

1. Create a Web site to introduce *The House of Mirth* to other readers. Design pages to intrigue and inform your audience, and invite other readers to post their thoughts and responses to their reading of the novel.

2. Write your own short story sequel to *The House of Mirth*. Imagine what Lawrence Selden's character will do after the death of Lily Bart. Will he change? Will he recognize that Gerty Farish loves him, reject the stuffy behavior of the wealthy class, and marry her?

3. Imagine you are the leader of a large, televised book club. You are interviewing Edith Wharton for your television audience. What questions would you ask?

CliffsNotes Resource Center

The learning doesn't need to stop here. CliffsNotes Resource Center shows you the best of the best—links to the best information in print and online about the author and related works. And don't think that this book is all we've prepared for you; we've put all kinds of pertinent information at www. cliffsnotes.com. Look for the terrific resources at your favorite bookstore or local library and on the Internet. When you're online, make your first stop www.cliffsnotes.com, where you'll find more incredibly useful information about *The House of Mirth,* including several bonus essays about the novel.

Books

This CliffsNotes book provides a meaningful interpretation of *The House of Mirth.* If you are looking for information about the author and related works, check out these other publications:

The Cambridge Companion to Edith Wharton, edited by respected Wharton scholar Millicent Bell, includes essays by prominent Wharton scholars that either directly or comparatively elucidate themes found in *The House of Mirth.* Cambridge University Press, Cambridge, U.K., 1995.

Edith Wharton, by Louis Auchincloss, celebrates Wharton's literary accomplishments, of which the author feels *The House of Mirth* is her first significant effort. University of Minnesota Press, Minneapolis, 1961.

Edith Wharton's Argument with America, by Elizabeth Ammons, includes the essay "Edith Wharton's Hard-Working Lily: *The House of Mirth* and the Marriage Market," in which Ammons places Wharton's novel within a genre of economic novels.

Edith Wharton: A Biography, by R. W. B. Lewis, includes extensive biographical detail on Wharton as she prepared to write *The House of Mirth,* which Lewis believed began as early as 1900, and proceeded in conception in 1903. Harper & Row, Publishers, Inc., New York, 1975.

A Feast of Words: The Triumph of Edith Wharton, by Cynthia Griffin Wolff, includes the essay "Lily Bart and the Beautiful Death," in which Wolff alternately supports and refutes Diana Trilling's thesis that the character of Lily Bart is a metaphor for the devaluation of art in the Gilded Age. Oxford University Press, New York, 1977.

"*The House of Mirth* Revisited," by Diana Trilling, depicts the character of Lily Bart as symbolic of artistic integrity, and presents Lily as embodying the elements of artistic virtue that the Gilded Age society rejects. Included in *Edith Wharton*, edited by Irving Howe, Englewood Cliffs, N.J., 1963.

If you're interested in other books published by Wiley Publishing, Inc., check out these Web sites:

- www.cliffsnotes.com
- www.dummies.com
- www.wiley.com

Magazines and Journals

Magazines and journals are excellent for additional information about *The House of Mirth* by Edith Wharton. You may want to check out these publications for information about the author and related works.

CONNELL, EILEEN. 1997. Edith Wharton Joins the Working Classes: *The House of Mirth* and the New York Working Girls' Clubs. *Women's Studies* 26, no. 6 (November): 557. Connell uses the character of Lily Bart to draw parallels between the feminist struggles of women in both the wealthy class and the working class at the turn of the century.

GERARD, BONNIE LYNN. 1998. From Tea to Chloral: Raising the Dead Lily Bart. Character in Woman Author Edith Wharton's book *The House of Mirth*. *Twentieth Century Literature*. 44, no. 4 (winter): 409. Gerard postulates that *The House of Mirth* is a novel about the conspicuous consumption of the Gilded Age wealthy socialites.

HOWE, IRVING. 1962. The Achievement of Edith Wharton. *Encounter* 19, no. 1 (July): 45–52. In a essay that compares all of Wharton's major fiction, Howe makes the assessment that Wharton was at her best when she handled moral issues in fixed social settings.

PAYNE, WILLIAM MORTON. 1906. Recent Fiction: *The House of Mirth*. *The Dial* XL, no. 469 (January): 15–16. Payne heralds Wharton as the preeminent female writer of her time, but ultimately dismisses the novel due to its "vain and vulgar" characters.

VON ROSK, NANCY. 2001. Spectacular Homes and Pastoral Theaters: Gender, Urbanity and Domesticity in *The House of Mirth*. *Studies in the Novel* 33, no. 3 (fall): 322. Von Rosk attempts to characterize Lily Bart as a logical extension and victim of the urban landscape in which she was raised and lived.

Internet

Check out these Web resources for more information about Edith Wharton and *The House of Mirth:*

Domestic Goddess: Edith Wharton, www.womenwriters.net/domestic goddess/wharton1.htm—An excellent overview of Wharton's life and works, including bio-critical sources.

Edith Wharton: An Overview with Biocritical Sources, www.geocities.com/ EnchantedForest/6741—Includes a chronology of Wharton's life and career, a list of her works, a picture gallery, biographical and critical sources, and links to other sites.

The Edith Wharton Society Home Page, http://guweb2.gonzaga.edu/ faculty/campbell/engl462/wharton.htm—Presents a biography of Wharton and links to sites with bibliographies and further information on Wharton and her literary works.

PAL: Perspectives in American Literature—A Research and Reference Guide, www.csustan.edu/english/reuben/pal/chap7/wharton.html— Contains an extensive bibliography of works on Wharton and her fiction.

Project Gutenberg, www.ibiblio.org/gutenberg/authors/wharton__ edith__1862-1937.html—Contains full texts of more than fifteen works by Wharton, including *The House of Mirth.*

Film and Other Recordings

The following films either adapt *The House of Mirth* or other novels by Edith Wharton that explore *The House of Mirth's* themes.

The Age of Innocence—Director Martin Scorsese's opulent and slow-moving 1993 adaptation of Wharton's novel concerns the plight of a society engagement that comes in the way of true love.

Ethan Frome—Less-than-successful 1993 cinematic adaptation of the Wharton novel stars Liam Neeson, Joan Allen, and Patricia Arquette.

The House of Mirth—As Lily Bart, actress Gillian Anderson won critical accolades in this 2000 film, which is perhaps the most faithful adaptation of a Wharton novel for the screen.

Index

NOTES